Java Programming: From Problem Analysis to Program Design, Third Edition Lab Manual

Blayne Mayfield

COURSE TECHNOLOGY
CENGAGE Learning

Australia • Brazil • Japan • Korea • Mexico • Singapore • Spain • United Kingdom • United States

COURSE TECHNOLOGY
CENGAGE Learning

Java Programming: From Problem Analysis to Program Design, Third Edition Lab Manual
Blayne Mayfield

Senior Product Manager: Alyssa Pratt

Acquisitions Editor: Amy Jollymore

Content Project Manager: Aimee Poirier

Editorial Assistant: Patrick Frank

Marketing Manager: Bryant Chrzan

Print Buyer: Julio Esperas

Compositor: GEX Publishing Services

Cover Designer: Lisa Buchanan-Kuhn, Curio Press, LLC

For product information and technology assistance, contact us at
Cengage Learning Customer & Sales Support, 1-800-354-9706

For permission to use material from this text or product, submit all requests online at **www.cengage.com/permissions**
Further permissions questions can be emailed to
permissionrequest@cengage.com

ISBN-13: 978-1-4239-0188-4

ISBN-10: 1-4239-0188-6

Course Technology
25 Thomson Place
Boston, Massachusetts 02210
USA

Cengage Learning is a leading provider of customized learning solutions with office locations around the globe, including Singapore, the United Kingdom, Australia, Mexico, Brazil, and Japan. Locate your local office at:
international.cengage.com/region

Cengage Learning products are represented in Canada by Nelson Education, Ltd.

To learn more about Course Technology, visit **www.cengage.com/coursetechnology**.

To learn more about Cengage Learning, visit **www.cengage.com**.

Purchase any of our products at your local bookstore or at our preferred online store **www.ichapters.com**.

Disclaimer
Course Technology reserves the right to revise this publication and make changes from time to time in its content without notice.

Printed in the United States of America
2 3 4 5 6 7 8 9 11 10 09 08

TABLE OF CONTENTS

INTRODUCTION

The objective of this lab manual is to give students step-by-step examples to become familiar with programming concepts, design, and coding. This text is designed to be used with *Java Programming: From Problem Analysis to Program Design, Third Edition*, but it also can be used to supplement any CS1 Java textbook. This manual is written to be used in a classroom lab environment.

FEATURES

To ensure a successful experience for instructors and students alike, this book includes the following features:

- **Lab Objectives**—Every lab has a brief description and list of learning objectives.
- **Materials Required**—Every lab includes information on hardware, software, and other materials you will need to complete the lab.
- **Completion Times**—Every lab has an estimated completion time so that you can plan your activities more accurately.
- **Activity Sections**—Labs are presented in manageable sections. Where appropriate, additional Activity Background information is provided to illustrate the importance of a particular project.
- **Step-by-Step Instructions**—Every lab provides steps to enhance technical proficiency; some labs include Critical Thinking exercises to challenge students.
- **Review Questions**—Some labs include review questions to help reinforce concepts presented in the lab.

SOFTWARE REQUIREMENTS

- Computer running Microsoft Windows ME, 2000, XP, or Vista
- Java 2 Standard Edition, Java Development Kit, v 6.0 (J2SE JDK 6.0), available on CD in the back of the main text. It is also available for download from *http://java.sun.com*

COMPLETING THE LAB ASSIGNMENTS

Some lab assignments require written answers to complete an exercise, while others are programming assignments that require you to work with a Java compiler.

- To complete the written assignments, remove the pages that your instructor assigns, and then write your answers directly on the pages of the Lab Manual.

- To complete the programming assignments, use the compiler that your instructor recommends or requires. Print all the documentation assigned, including program code, program prompts, input, and output displayed on the screen, input files, and output files. You can submit your written answers and the printed documentation with a lab cover sheet for grading.

  If your instructor requires an electronic copy of your work, e-mail the completed assignment to your instructor or include removable media (e.g., CD-R or flash drive) with your work. Your instructor will tell you what is needed, but be sure to submit the .java, .class, and any .dat or .txt files that you create, as well as any input and output files. Also include your name or ID in the titles of all your files.

- To provide program documentation, compile and run your program, copy the prompts, input, and output (if appropriate), and paste them as a block comment at the end of your program.

  In Windows 2000, click the Mark button on the toolbar of the output window. (The toolbar appears by default; if the output window does not have a toolbar, follow the instructions for Windows XP.) Drag to select the text you want to copy, and then click the Copy button. Open your program in a text editor, click at the end of the program, and type /* to begin a block comment. Press Ctrl+V to paste the text in the program file, and then type */ to end the block comment.

  In Windows XP or Vista, right-click the title bar of the output window, point to Edit, and then click Mark. Drag to select the text you want to copy, and then press Enter. Open your program in a text editor, click at the end of the program, and type /* to begin a block comment. Press Ctrl+V to paste the text in the program file, and then type */ to end the block comment.

  After you paste the comment in the program, either print the program file from your text editor or submit the program file to your instructor electronically.

ABOUT THE AUTHOR

Blayne Mayfield joined the faculty of the Computer Science Department at Oklahoma State University in 1988. His research interests are object-oriented computing, artificial intelligence, and computer graphics. He earned his Ph.D. in Computer Science from the University of Missouri - Rolla.

ACKNOWLEDGMENTS

I would like to thank my family for their support, and for giving up time with me so that I could pursue this project. I also thank the editorial staff of Course Technology, and those who reviewed the materials found in this manual.

Sincere thanks and acknowledgements go to Dr. Judy Scholl for her work on the first edition of this Lab Manual.

AN OVERVIEW OF COMPUTERS AND PROGRAMMING LANGUAGES

In this chapter, you will:

♦ Learn about different types of computers

♦ Explore the hardware and software components of a computer system

♦ Learn about the language of a computer

♦ Learn about the evolution of programming languages

♦ Examine high-level programming languages

♦ Discover what a compiler is and what it does

♦ Examine how a Java program is processed

♦ Learn what an algorithm is and explore problem-solving techniques

♦ Become aware of structured design and object-oriented design programming methodologies

CHAPTER 1: ASSIGNMENT COVER SHEET

Name _____   Date _____

Section _____

Lab Assignments	Grade
Lab 1.1 Identifying Different Types of Computers	
Lab 1.2 Identifying and Defining Hardware and Software Components	
Lab 1.3 Storing Information Electronically	
Lab 1.4 Processing a Java Program	
Lab 1.5 Programming with the Problem Analysis-Coding-Execution Cycle	
Lab 1.6 Object-Oriented Programming	
Total Grade	

See your instructor or the introduction to this book for instructions on submitting your assignments.

LAB 1.1 IDENTIFYING DIFFERENT TYPES OF COMPUTERS

Computers have evolved from their introduction in the 1950s, when there were very few computers, through the 1960s, when manufacturers produced very large, expensive computers, to the 1970s, when people began to use cheaper, smaller computers. By the 1990s, the affordability of microcomputers made them common in homes and small businesses. The mainframe, midsized, and microcomputers of today are much faster than ever before. Regardless of their size, speed, or cost, all types of computers share basic elements, including input, output, storage, and performance of arithmetic and logical operations.

A mainframe computer was once one of the largest, fastest, and most powerful computers available. However, a mainframe in 1960 was less powerful than today's microcomputer. A midsized computer was less expensive, less powerful, and smaller than a mainframe, and was created as a more affordable alternative to mainframes. Today, the microcomputer is called the personal computer. Personal computers are usually advertised with descriptions of their features clearly stated to help nonspecialist consumers match the features with their needs.

As the twenty-first century marches on, personal computers continue to become faster, smaller, and less costly. Handheld computers and personal data assistants (PDAs) make it possible for people to take their computers with them when they are away from home or the office. The widespread availability of wireless networks permits these "mobile computers" to communicate with one another and with other computers. Many manufacturers have even incorporated personal computer or PDA functionality into cellular telephones.

Objectives

In this lab, you become acquainted with the different types of computers that have evolved and identify how these types are used.

After completing this lab, you will be able to:

- Identify and define the different types of computers.

- Identify the different uses of the different types of computers.

Estimated completion time: **10–15 minutes**

Identifying Different Types of Computers

Match the following terms with the appropriate definitions.

1. _____ 1950s

2. _____ 1990s

3. _____ 2000s

4. _____ Ada Augusta

5. _____ Mainframe

6. _____ Midsized computer

7. _____ Microcomputer

a) One of the largest, fastest, and most powerful computers, until recently

b) When computers became affordable for nonspecialists

c) A computer less expensive and smaller than a mainframe that allowed more companies to afford computers

d) Personal computer

e) When computers were introduced to very few people

f) Widely considered to be the first computer programmer

g) When mobile computing became commonly available

Lab 1.2 Identifying and Defining Hardware and Software Components

A computer is made up of physical components (hardware) and programs (software). You should be able to identify these elements of a computer system and understand and define terminology used to describe a computer system.

Objectives

In this lab, you become acquainted with common computer terminology regarding hardware and software components.

After completing this lab, you will be able to:

- Identify and define hardware components.
- Distinguish between types of programs.
- Recognize addressing, storage, input, and output.

Estimated completion time: **15–20 minutes**

Identifying and Defining Hardware Components

Match the following terms with the appropriate definitions.

1. _____ Secondary storage

    a) An electronic device that can perform commands to input, output, or store data, and can calculate arithmetic and logical expressions

2. _____ Address

    b) Computer components including the central processing unit (CPU), main memory (MM), input/output devices, and secondary storage

3. _____ Arithmetic logic unit

    c) The brain of the computer, containing several components such as the control unit (CU), program counter (PC), instruction register (IR), arithmetic logic unit (ALU), and accumulator (ACC)

4. _____ Computer

    d) Also known as RAM, or Random Access Memory

5. _____ CPU

    e) Points to the next instruction to be executed

6. _____ Main memory

    f) Holds the instruction that is currently being executed

7. _____ Hardware

    g) Devices including monitor, printer, and secondary storage

8. _____ Input devices

    h) The component of the CPU that performs arithmetic and logical operations

9. _____ Instruction register

    i) A unique location in main memory

10. _____ Output devices

    j) Stores information permanently

11. _____ Program counter

    k) Devices including keyboard, mouse, and secondary storage

Identifying and Defining Software Components

Match the following terms with the appropriate definitions.

1. _____ Application program

2. _____ Program

3. _____ Software

4. _____ System program

a) Computer instructions to solve a problem

b) There are two types: system and application

c) Controls the computer

d) Performs a specific task; examples include word processors, spreadsheets, and games

Answer questions about the computer you use in your computer lab:

1. What is the operating system of the computer you use?

2. How much main memory does the computer you use have?

3. What output devices are connected to the computer you use?

4. How much secondary storage does the computer you use have?

To give you an idea of how far computer technology has progressed, search the World Wide Web to answer questions about ENIAC, the first electronic, general-purpose computer:

1. When and where was ENIAC built?

2. ENIAC was not a "stored program" computer. How was it programmed?

3. How many arithmetic operations per second could ENIAC perform?

4. How large was ENIAC?

LAB 1.3 STORING INFORMATION ELECTRONICALLY

A computer is an electronic device that processes digital signals, which represent information as binary numbers. A binary number is a sequence of bits (0s and 1s). All data is stored and manipulated on a computer as binary numbers.

Objectives

In this lab, you become acquainted with electronic signals and the representative code used to interpret these signals.

After completing this lab, you will be able to:

- Identify the machine representation of computer code.

Estimated completion time: **15–20 minutes**

Storing Information Electronically

Fill in each blank with the appropriate term.

1. _____ signals represent information as a continuous waveform.

2. _____ signals represent information with a sequence of 0s and 1s.

3. The ASCII encoding scheme can represent _____ different characters, whereas the Unicode encoding scheme can represent _____ different characters.

4. The digits 0 and 1 are called _____ or the shortened term _____ .

5. The sequence of 0s and 1s is referred to as _____ .

6. A sequence of eight bits is called a(n) _____ .

7. The most common text-encoding scheme on personal computers is _____ _____ and is abbreviated as _____ .

8. The ASCII character represented by the decimal number 97 is _____ .

9. The ASCII character represented by the decimal number 65 is _____ .

10. A gigabyte is equivalent to _____ megabytes.

11. Java differentiates between uppercase and lowercase characters. True or false? _____

12. Early computers using machine language that used binary code made programming prone to errors. True or false? _____

13. Assembly language uses _____ to make instructions easy to remember.

14. A program that translates assembly language instructions into machine language is called a(n) _____ .

15. A program that translates instructions written in a high-level language into machine code is called a(n) _____ .

Give the decimal representations of the following integers and ASCII characters:

1. 'A'

2. 4

3. '4'

4. 'a'

5. '\n'

6. '\0'

7. 0

8. '0'

LAB 1.4 PROCESSING A JAVA PROGRAM

Java is one of many programming languages that are high-level languages, which makes it closer to a natural language than machine language and assembly language. To run on a computer, Java instructions first need to be translated into an intermediate language called bytecode and then interpreted into a particular machine language. A program called a compiler translates instructions written in Java into bytecode. Java programs and their bytecode translations are machine independent, meaning that they can run on many different types of computer platforms.

There are two types of Java programs—applications and applets. Four steps are necessary to execute a program written in Java:

- You use a text editor to create a program that is called the source program. The program must be saved in a text file named *ClassName*.java, where *ClassName* is the name of the Java class contained in the file.

- The program is checked for syntax errors by another program called a compiler. When the program is syntactically correct, the compiler translates the program into bytecode and saves it in a file with the .class extension.

- To run a Java application program, the .class file must be loaded into the computer's memory. To run a Java applet program, it must be loaded using a Web browser or applet viewer. Java programs generally are written with the aid of a software development kit (SDK), which is a suite of programs and libraries that support program development and execution. The Java library included in the SDK is a set of packages, where each package contains a collection of prewritten, related classes that have been tested thoroughly. An SDK program called a *linker* connects the bytecode of your program with that of the library classes used by your program.

- To execute the Java program, the linked code needs to be loaded in the main memory. This is accomplished by a program called a loader. Finally, a program called an interpreter translates each bytecode instruction into the machine language of your computer, and then executes it.

Objectives

In this lab, you become acquainted with the different programs in the SDK that are needed to process a source program written in a high-level language program.

After completing this lab, you will be able to:

- Identify the process needed to convert a high-level language program to an executable program.

Estimated completion time: **10–15 minutes**

```
                        ┌──────────┐
                        │ Problem  │
                        └──────────┘
                        ┌──────────┐
                        │          │
                        └──────────┘
                        ┌──────────┐
                        │          │
                        └──────────┘
                        ┌──────────┐
                        │          │
                        └──────────┘
                        ┌──────────┐
                        │ Compiler │
        ┌──────────┐    └──────────┘
        │ Library  │    ┌──────────┐
        └──────────┘    │ Bytecode │
                        └──────────┘
                        ┌──────────┐
                        │  Loader  │
                        └──────────┘
                        ┌──────────────┐
                        │ Interpreter  │
                        └──────────────┘
                        ┌──────────┐
                        │          │
                        └──────────┘
```

3. What is the most important step in program development? Why?

4. Why would you break a problem into subproblems during the analysis step?

5. After analyzing a problem to be solved, you design an algorithm for each subproblem. What is an algorithm?

6. Converting your design into a high-level language only occurs after your design has been checked to confirm it is logically sound. What steps do you take after you have created your source code from your design?

7. Even if a program executes successfully, how do you know that it is correct?

8. Consider the problem of converting temperatures from Fahrenheit to centigrade. To perform the conversion, you first subtract 32 from the Fahrenheit temperature, and then multiply the result by 5/9.

Write the algorithm to find the centigrade temperature equivalent to any given Fahrenheit temperature.

BASIC ELEMENTS OF JAVA

In this chapter, you will:

♦ Become familiar with the basic components of a Java program, including methods, special symbols, and identifiers

♦ Explore primitive data types

♦ Discover how to use arithmetic operators

♦ Examine how a program evaluates arithmetic expressions

♦ Explore how mixed expressions are evaluated

♦ Learn about type casting

♦ Become familiar with the `String` type

♦ Learn what an assignment statement is and what it does

♦ Discover how to input data into memory by using input statements

♦ Become familiar with the use of increment and decrement operators

♦ Examine ways to output results using output statements

♦ Learn how to import packages and why they are necessary

♦ Discover how to create a Java application program

♦ Explore how to properly structure a program, including using comments to document a program

CHAPTER 2: ASSIGNMENT COVER SHEET

Name _____   Date _____

Section _____

Lab Assignments	Grade
Lab 2.1 Identifying Basic Elements of a Java Program	
Lab 2.2 Identifying Data Types	
Lab 2.3 Using Arithmetic Operators	
Lab 2.4 Using the class String	
Lab 2.5 Allocating Memory, Writing Assignment Statements, and Writing Input Statements	
Lab 2.6 Using Strings, Writing to the Screen, Using Common Escape Sequences, and Using the Method flush	
Lab 2.7 Using Packages, Classes, Methods, and the Import Statement to Write a Java Program Using Good Programming Style and Form (Critical Thinking Exercises)	
Total Grade	

See your instructor or the introduction to this book for instructions on submitting your assignments.

LAB 2.1 IDENTIFYING BASIC ELEMENTS OF A JAVA PROGRAM

A computer program is a sequence of statements that work together to accomplish some task. Recall that there are two types of Java programs—*applications* and *applets*. The main focus of this book is Java application programming. To write meaningful programs, you must learn the special symbols, words, and syntax rules of any programming language. You must also learn semantic rules, which determine the meaning of the instructions. In addition, you should learn the *tokens*, which are the smallest units of a program written in any programming language. Java tokens are divided into special symbols, word symbols, and identifiers.

Following are some special symbols in Java:

```
+    -      *     /

.    ;      ?     ,

<=   !=     ==    >=
```

Some Java *word symbols* (also called *reserved words* or *keywords*) are `int`, `float`, `double`, `char`, `void`, `public`, `static`, `throws`, and `return`.

Identifiers are simply names. Some identifiers are predefined; others are defined by the programmer. A Java identifier can only consist of letters, digits, the underscore character (_), and the dollar sign character ($). Identifiers cannot start with a digit and are case sensitive. Although identifiers can be of any length, each computer system sets a maximum for the number of significant characters it processes, which restricts the length of an identifier. Furthermore, the programmer cannot define identifiers that have the same name as the word symbols.

Objectives

In this lab, you become acquainted with tokens, which are the special symbols, word symbols, and identifiers used in Java statements.

After completing this lab, you will be able to:

- Recognize special symbols.
- Recognize word symbols.
- Recognize identifiers.
- Recognize invalid symbol representations.

Estimated completion time: **15–20 minutes**

Identifying Basic Elements of a Java Program

Indicate whether each of the following representations is a special symbol, word symbol, identifier, or is invalid. If a token is invalid, briefly state why it is invalid.

Token	Special symbol	Word symbol	Identifier	Invalid
1. static				
2. #ofRooms				
3. double				
4. $10				
5. $10,000				
6. ab*				
7. return				
8. c3po				
9. Void				
10. 123z				
11. ?				
12. integer				
13. qr&				
14. first name				
15. *				
16. R2D2				
17. 5days				
18. !=				
19. +xy				
20. hello				

Lab 2.4 Using the Class String

Values that can contain more than one character are called *strings* and use the class name `String`. Strictly speaking, a string is a sequence of zero or more characters, and strings are not a primitive type in Java. A string containing no characters is called a *null* or *empty string*. In Java, strings are enclosed in double quotation marks. To process strings effectively, Java provides the class `String`, which contains various operations to manipulate strings.

Each character in a string has a position relative to the beginning of the string. The position of the first character in a string is 0, the position of the second character is 1, and so on. The length of a string is the number of characters in it. Remember that a space is a character, so spaces count toward the length of a string.

Objectives

In this lab, you learn to calculate the length of strings and the positions of specific characters within strings.

After completing this lab, you will be able to:

- Calculate the length of strings and character positions of specific characters within strings.

Estimated completion time: **15–20 minutes**

Using the Class String

Calculate the length of each of the following strings.

String expression	String length
1. "Tuesday, January 1, 2008"	
2. "6.0E-23"	
3. "2 + 2 = 4"	
4. "a b c...xyz"	
5. ""	

Calculate the positions of all occurrences of the specified character within the following strings.

String expression	All positions
1. "Tuesday, January 1, 2008", character 'r'	
2. "6.0E-23", character '2'	
3. "2 + 2 = 4", character '4'	
4. "a b c...xyz", character '.'	
5. "Java reserved words", character ' ' (space)	

Lab 2.5 Allocating Memory, Writing Assignment Statements, and Writing Input Statements

When you allocate memory in a computer program, you specify a name to identify each memory location being allocated. In addition, you indicate the type of data that will be stored in those memory locations. A memory location that has an unchangeable value is called a *named constant*. It is customary for all letters in the identifier (name) of a named constant to be uppercase letters. Using uppercase characters for named constants is not required, but doing so makes it easy to distinguish constants from the identifiers of memory locations whose values can be changed. Because named constants do not change their values, they must be initialized at declaration. You declare a memory location as a named constant with the following syntax:

```
static final  dataType identifier = value;
```

In Java, `static` and `final` are reserved words. The word `final` specifies that the value stored in the memory location is fixed and cannot be changed. The word `static` is optional, depending on the circumstance.

In Java, memory locations that can be changed are called *variable memory locations* or *variables*. Variables can be initialized at declaration and can be given different values throughout execution. You declare a variable with the following syntax:

dataType identifier1, identifier2, ..., identifierN;

Data is stored in a variable either through an assignment statement or through an input (read) statement. *Assignment* statements use the = (assignment) operator. Java evaluates the expression to the right of the assignment operator and stores the result in the memory address identified by the variable to the left of the operator. The result of the expression on the right must be a value compatible with the data type of the variable on the left. The first time a value is placed in the variable is called *initialization*. Tracing values through a sequence of statements—called a *walk-through* or *desk check*—is a valuable tool to learn and practice.

In Java, using a variable without initializing it causes a compile-time error unless it is a class variable; in the latter case, the default value associated with the data type is assigned automatically to the variable.

When the computer receives data from the keyboard, the user is said to be *acting interactively*. In Java, you insert data into variables from the *standard input device* (usually, the keyboard) by using the predefined standard input stream object, `System.in`. Data is extracted in the form of characters from the input stream. Many times, though, you want to read data into integer, floating-point, or string variables. You can read data directly into variables of these types by creating and using an object of the predefined Java class `Scanner`, as follows:

```
static Scanner console = new Scanner(System.in);
```

To read a string value from an input stream, you can use the `Scanner` method `next`, as demonstrated by the following statement:

```
String oneWord = console.next();
```

For example, assume that the input stream consists of the data "`January 1 is on \nTuesday`". Then, the preceding statement reads the token "`January`" from the standard input stream, `System.in`, and assigns it to the variable `oneWord`. (A *token* is a sequence of characters separated from other tokens by *white space*—spaces, tabs, newlines, and carriage returns.)

You can read an integer value from an input stream by calling the `Scanner` method `nextInt`, as shown in the following statement:

```
int numOfDays = console.nextInt();
```

In this statement, `nextInt` reads a token from the standard input stream and converts it to an `int` value, and then the value is stored into the variable `numOfDays`. If this statement follows the earlier call to `next`, the value 18 is stored into `numOfDays`. A similar method that can be used to read floating-point values is `nextDouble`.

Another method for reading string values is `nextLine`, which retrieves data from an input stream until a newline character is read. For example, if a call to `nextLine` follows the earlier call to `nextInt`, the string " is on" is read and returned. (Note the leading blank is part of the string.)

Sometimes, you may want to retrieve a single-character response from the standard input stream. (For example, you might prompt the user with, "Enter 'y' to continue or 'n' to quit".) This can be accomplished as shown in this statement:

```
char response = console.next().charAt(0);
```

First, the method `next` reads a token from the standard input stream, and then the `String` method `charAt` is called for that token. The method `charAt` retrieves the character located at the specified position within the string; in this case, the first character of the string (the character at position 0) is retrieved. Finally, the character is assigned to the variable `response`.

Variables can obtain values either through input or through assignment. Inputting data offers the program more flexibility and usually involves a prompt to tell the user to enter the data. Assignments are used in calculations. The *increment* (++) and *decrement* (--) operators are used in assignment statements or with the variable name alone to increase or decrease a variable by one.

Objectives

In this lab, you learn that allocating memory with both variables and named constants results in the program assigning a name and type to the memory location. You must initialize named constants when you declare them; initialization is optional for variables, but they must be given a value before they can be used. In addition, you learn that the value of variables can be changed through assignment or inputting data. When you want to increase or decrease the value of a variable by 1, you can use the increment or decrement operator, respectively.

After completing this lab, you will be able to:

- Allocate memory with both variables and named constants.
- Assign values to variables when expressions are evaluated.
- Assign values to variables through input.
- Use the decrement and increment operators.

Estimated completion time: **30 minutes**

Allocating Memory, Writing Assignment Statements, and Writing Input Statements

Describe the following declarations, assignments, and input statements. Indicate the value in memory after each statement is executed. Write "invalid" if a statement contains an error and briefly state why.

Statements	The variable name and value of each statement
1. `int a = 12, b;` `b = a;`	
2. `double x = 5, y = 1.5;` `x = x + y;`	
3. `short a = 21; b = 7;`	

4. `short number = 0;`
`number = 10;`
`number = (short)(number + 5);`
 	
What occurs if your statement is:
`number = number + 5;`	

5. `double value = 32.5;`
`int delta = 2;`
`value = value + delta;`	

6. `final int SQUARE = 9;`	

7. `double x = -14.5, y = 22.5;`
`int d = 3;`
`y = d - x + y;`	

8. `final double RESULT = 4.0;` `RESULT = RESULT * 2;`	

9. `int n;`
`double d;`
`// The user should be asked`
`// for a value here.`
`// Assume the user enters`
`// '-3 47.25'.`
`n = console.nextInt();`
`d = console.nextDouble();`	

10. `String s;`[new line]`int i;`
`// The user should be asked`
`// for a value here.`
`// Assume the user enters`
`// 'apple pie'.`
`s = console.next();`
`i = console.nextInt();`	

11. `String x, y;`
`// The user should be asked`
`// for a value here.`
`// Assume the user enters`
`// 'Gas - Next Exit'.`
`x = console.next();`
`y = console.nextLine();`	

Statements	The variable name and value of each statement

12. `char c;`
`// The user should be asked`
`// for a single-character`
`// value here.`
`// Assume the user enters`
`// 'A'.`
`c = console.next().charAt(0);`	

13. `double a, b, c = 0.0;`	
14. `int d = 2, x = 3, y = 4;` `4 = d - x + y;`	

15. `double mean = 12.5;`
`double range = 3.0;`
`int max = mean + range / 2;`	

16. `int b = 9.0;`	

17. `int num1 = 8, num2 = 3,`
`      temp;`
`temp = num1;`
`num1 = num2;`
`num2 = temp;`	

18. `int num;`
`// The user should be asked`
`// for a value here.`
`// Assume the user enters 8.`
`num = console.nextInt();`
`num++;`
`num++;`	

19. `int c = 8, d = 6, e = 2;`
`c = c - e++;`
`d = d + --e;`	

20. `double x = 5.0;`
`int y = 4;`
`x = x + y / 4;`	

21. `double x = 5.0;`
`int y = 4;`
`y = x + y/4;`	

LAB 2.6 USING STRINGS, WRITING TO THE SCREEN, USING COMMON ESCAPE SEQUENCES, AND USING THE METHOD flush

When used with two numeric operands, the + operator adds their values. When used with two string operands, the + operator concatenates the strings. When used with a string and a character or numeric, the + operator implicitly converts the character or numeric to a string value and concatenates it with the other string. For example, the expression:

```
"Your score is " + 97
```

is equivalent to the expression:

```
"Your score is  " + "97"
```

In Java, programs usually produce output on the *standard output device*, System.out. You can use three methods, print, println, and printf, to output a string on the standard output device. These methods are used to form output statements. (printf is covered in the next chapter.) The expression that appears in an output statement is evaluated and its value is displayed beginning at the current cursor position on the output device. The method print repositions the cursor immediately after the last character printed. The method println positions the cursor at the beginning of the next line. For example, the statements:

```
System.out.print("Harvest");
System.out.println("Moon");
System.out.println("Dance");
```

display:

```
HarvestMoon
Dance
```

and the cursor is placed at the beginning of a new line following the word "Dance".

You also can embed a newline escape sequence ('\n') within the expression to be printed to move the cursor to the beginning of the next line before printing the portion of the expression value following the newline. The '\n' can be written as a character by itself or within a string. For example, this statement:

```
System.out.println("HarvestMoon\nDance");
```

produces the same output as the three statements in the previous example.

When writing a long string value using a print or println statement, you can break the string into multiple pieces and use the + concatenation operator to continue the output statement on the next line. This makes your program much easier to read and maintain. If the string you break up is a sentence, remember to include blanks after the last word of one piece or before the first word of the next piece.

Most *escape sequences* are used to control output formatting, and some are more commonly used than others. In addition to newline, other escape sequences are available, including the following:

- The tab (\t), which moves the cursor to the next tab stop

- The backspace (\b), which moves the cursor one space to the left

- The carriage return (\r), which moves the cursor back to the beginning of the current line (not the next line)

- The backslash (\\), which allows a backslash to be printed

- The single quotation, (\'), which allows the single quotation to be printed

- The double quotation (\"), which allows the double quotation to be printed

LAB 2.7 USING PACKAGES, CLASSES, METHODS, AND THE IMPORT STATEMENT TO WRITE A JAVA PROGRAM USING GOOD PROGRAMMING STYLE AND FORM

Java provides a collection of related, prewritten, pretested classes in libraries, called *packages*; these classes define the methods, operators, and identifiers needed to run a Java application or applet. You can think of a method as a named sequence of instructions designed to accomplish a specific task. The package `java.io` contains classes for inputting data into a program and outputting the results of a program.

To indicate that your program uses a given class from a package, include an *import* statement for the class. This import statement specifies the name of the package and the name of the class, separated by the dot operator. If many classes from the same package are used by your program, you either can include import statements for each of the classes used, or you can include a single statement that imports all classes contained in the package. The latter import statement specifies the name of the package and an asterisk ('`*`'), separated by the dot operator. For example, here is a statement that imports the class `Scanner` from the package `java.util` and a statement that imports all classes from the package `java.io`:

```
import java.util.Scanner;
import java.io.*;
```

A program written using the Java syntax, or grammar rules, is called *Java source code*; such a program consists of a collection of imported classes and classes written by the programmer. The package `java.lang` is imported into the program implicitly, meaning that you don't have to include an import statement to use its classes. That package contains the commonly used methods `print` and `println`. Generally, each class the programmer writes is stored in a separate file, and the names of these files must end with the `.java` extension. Moreover, the name of the class and the part of its filename that precedes the extension must be the same. Every Java application program must contain a method named `main`.

The method `main` must follow the Java syntax and consists of a heading and a body. The body of the program consists of a sequence of zero or more statements enclosed in curly braces. Declaration statements are those used to declare elements such as variables. Executable statements perform calculations, manipulate data, create output, accept input, and so on. Java programs must follow not only Java syntax but also Java semantics, which is the set of rules that applies meaning to statements and operations. For ease of use, programs should be well-documented using both comments and meaningful identifier names, and they should have an easy-to-read format using indentation and strategically placed blank lines.

Comments document a program by explaining its purpose, identifying who wrote the program, and explaining the purpose of particular statements. Single-line comments begin with // anywhere on the line; everything encountered on that line after // is ignored by the compiler as a comment. Multiple-line comments are enclosed between /* and */.

Using meaningful identifier names and making them easily readable are other ways to document a program. Many Java programmers employ *camelback notation* to name variables, in which the words that make up an identifier name use lowercase letters, except for the letters that begin the second, third, and subsequent words. Examples of camelback identifier names are `hatSize` and `numberOfDays`. Other programmers use no uppercase letters in identifier names, but separate the words with the underscore character (_), instead. Examples of this notation are `hat_size` and `number_of_days`. Most Java programmers choose constant names that contain no lowercase letters and in which words are separated by underscores. Examples of such constant names include `CIRCLE_RADIUS` and `NEAREST_POINT`. The examples in this book follow these standards.

Another important documentation tool is to provide clearly written prompts to inform the user how to interact correctly with a program.

In addition to simple assignment statements, you can use a compound assignment statement for more concise notation. The compound operators are +=, -=, *=, /=, and %=.

Objectives

In this lab, you learn to write complete programs with Java import statements.

After completing this lab, you will be able to:

- Read a complete program and determine the output.

- Write a complete program including import statements for input/output and strings.

- Use a readable format in a Java program.

- Use meaningful identifiers.

- Use comments for documentation.

Estimated completion time: **60–80 minutes**

Using Packages, Classes, Methods, and the Import Statement to Write a Java Program Using Good Programming Style and Form

Describe the following program declarations, assignments, input, and output statements. Indicate how the values in memory have changed after each statement is executed. Show what is displayed after each output statement or write Java code to implement the comment statements or program design. Use an editor to enter the programs. From the command line, compile and execute the programs. Then compare your work to the actual output of your programs.

1. Describe the following program, including the use of import statements when necessary. Show what is displayed as output. Then, enter and execute the program in a file named StuInfo1.java. Save your source code to the device or location specified by your instructor.

   To compile your program from the command line, type javac followed by the name of your program using the .java extension, as in javac StuInfo1.java. Correct any errors until your program compiles.

   To execute your program from the command line, type java followed by the name of your program with no extension, as in java StuInfo1.

   After your program is executed, copy the output and save it in a block comment at the end of your program.

```
import java.util.Scanner;

public class StuInfo1
{

  public static void main(String[] args)
  {
    Scanner console = new Scanner(System.in);

    String first_name, last_name, classification, major;
    double gpa;

    System.out.print("Please enter your first name: ");
    first_name = console.nextLine();
```

```
em.out.print("Please enter your last name: ");
_name = console.nextLine();

em.out.print("Please enter your classification:\n"
    + "freshman, sophomore, junior, senior, special, "
    + "or graduate: ");
ssification = console.next();

tem.out.print("Please enter your major abbreviation: ");
or = console.next();

stem.out.print("Please enter your grade point average: ");
a = console.nextDouble();

stem.out.println("\nYou have entered the following "
    + "information:\n"
    + "\nName:\t\t" + first_name + ' ' + last_name
    + "\nClassification:\t" + classification
    + "\nMajor:\t\t" + major
    + "\ngpa:\t\t" + gpa);
}
```

2. a   Design a Java program that prompts the user to select a lunch from several sandwich choices. The user should be prompted with the following information:

- Identification of the program and an explanation of how to use it

- Sandwich choices: Ham, Beef, Reuben, PBJ, Cheese, or Vegetarian

- Bread choices: Rye, Wheat, White, Sourdough, or Pumpernickel

- Condiment choices: Mayo, Mustard, Ketchup, or none

- Drink choices: Coke, Diet, Tea, Coffee, Water

- The price of a half sandwich or a whole sandwich: 3.99 or 5.99

Then, the user enters his choices for each of the menu items.

After all data has been entered, display the selection. Be sure to leave blank lines for readability, and include comments to identify the program author, to describe the program, and to describe program statements. You need the import statement for input. Use Lab 2.7, Exercise 1 as a guideline for designing the code.

Write your design in the following space. Your design should be a list of Java comments without any code.

b.   Write a Java program based on the design you created in Exercise 2a. Enter the program into a file named Deli.java, save the file, compile the program, and execute it. After your program is executed, copy the output and save it in a block comment at the end of your program. Save your source code to the device or location specified by your instructor.

The following is a copy of the screen results that might appear after running your program, depending on the data entered. The input entered by the user appears in bold.

```
Welcome to the Sandwich Corral


You will be given choices for building your sandwich.
Please enter your selection after each prompt
and then press the Enter key.


Please enter your sandwich choice.
Ham, Beef, Reuben, PBJ, Cheese, or Vegetarian: Ham
Please enter your bread selection.
Rye, Wheat, White, Sourdough, or Pumpernickel: Rye
Please enter your choice of condiment (one only).
Mayo, Mustard, Ketchup, none: Mustard
Please enter your drink choice.
Coke, Diet, Tea, Coffee, or Water: Water
Please enter 3.99 for a half sandwich or 5.99
for a whole sandwich: 3.99


You have entered the following information:

Sandwich:       Ham
Bread:          Rye
Condiment:      Mustard
Drink:          Water

Tab:            3.99
```

3. a. *Critical Thinking Exercise*: Design a complete Java program that asks the user for two names. Display the two names the user enters—this is called *echo printing*. Swap the values of the names. For example, name1 will become name2, and name2 will become name1. Display the two names after they have been swapped. Use Lab 2.5, Exercise 16 for reference.

After all data has been entered and the names have been swapped, display the values of the names. Be sure to leave blank lines for readability and comments to identify the program author, to describe the program, and to describe program statements. You need the import statement for input and output.

Write your design in the following space. Your design should be a list of Java comments without any code.

3. b. Write a Java program based on the design you created in Exercise 3a. Enter the program into a file named `Swap.java`, save the file, compile the program, and execute it. After your program is executed, copy the output and save it in a block comment at the end of your program. Save your source code to the device or location specified by your instructor.

Following is a copy of the screen results that might appear after running your program, depending on the data entered. The input entered by the user appears in bold.

```
You will be asked to enter two names.
The program will display the names you entered, swap
the names, and then display them after they are swapped.

Please enter the first name: Romeo
Please enter the second name: Juliet
You entered Romeo as your first name and Juliet as your
second name.

After swapping the names,
the first name is Juliet
and the second name is Romeo.
```

4. a. *Critical Thinking Exercise*: Imagine that you and your band have just recorded a song, and you want to permit fans to purchase and download the song over the Internet. Your manager receives a commission equal to 12% of the total sales revenue for your song, and the Internet site that lists your song receives a 3% commission. Design a Java program that asks the user for the title of the song, the purchase price of the song (in dollars and cents), and the number of copies of the song that have been sold. Calculate the total revenue generated by your song, the commission received by your manager, and the commission received by the Internet site. Use named constants for the commission rates.

Write your design in the following space. Your design should be a list of Java comments without any code.

4. b. Write a Java program based on the design you created in Exercise 4a. Enter the program into a file named `SongSales.java`, save the file, compile the program, and execute it. After your program is executed, copy the output and save it in a block comment at the end of your program. Save your source code to the device or location specified by your instructor.

The following is a copy of the screen results that might appear after running your program, depending on the data entered. The input entered by the user appears in bold.

```
This program calculates the revenue earned and commission paid for a
song sold over the Internet.
```

Please enter the name of the song: **The Beginning of Time**
Please enter the selling price in dollars and cents: **0.89**
Please enter the number of copies sold: **100000**

100000 copies of the song "The Beginning of Time" were sold at $0.89
per copy, for a total revenue of $89000.0

The commission received by your agent is $10680.0
The commission received by the Internet site is $2670.0

CHAPTER

3

INTRODUCTION TO OBJECTS AND INPUT/OUTPUT

In this chapter, you will:

- ♦ Learn about objects and reference variables
- ♦ Explore how to use predefined methods in a program
- ♦ Become familiar with the class `String`
- ♦ Explore how to format output using the method `printf`
- ♦ Learn how to use input and output dialog boxes in a program
- ♦ Become familiar with the `String` method `format`
- ♦ Become familiar with file input and output

41

CHAPTER 3: ASSIGNMENT COVER SHEET

Name   Date

Section _____

Lab Assignments	Grade
Lab 3.1 Examining Objects and Reference Variables, Using the Predefined Class Math and the pow Method	
Lab 3.2 Using the String Class	
Lab 3.3 Formatting Numeric Data, Parsing Numeric Strings, and Using Dialog Boxes for Input and Output (Critical Thinking Exercises)	
Lab 3.4 Using Files for Input and Output (Critical Thinking Exercises)	
Total Grade	

See your instructor or the introduction to this book for instructions on submitting your assignments.

LAB 3.2 USING THE String CLASS

Recall that `String` variables are reference variables. When you assign a string value to a `String` variable, the variable actually contains the memory location of the `String` object that contains the string value. The class `String` is part of the Java system. As you saw earlier, a `String` variable or object can be used to invoke a `String` method using the dot operator, the method name, and the arguments (if any) required by the method.

A string is a sequence of zero or more characters. The position of the first character is 0, the position of the second character is 1, and so on.

Before outputting numeric data, a Java program first converts numeric data to strings, which the program then displays or prints.

Objectives

In this lab, you learn to use methods of the `String` class.

After completing this lab, you will be able to use the following methods:

- `String`
- `indexOf`
- `concat`
- `length`
- `substring`
- `toLowerCase`
- `toUpperCase`

Estimated completion time: **40–50 minutes**

Using the String Class

Design and write a complete Java program based on the following instructions and output example.

1. a. Design a Java program that assigns the string values "Hi" and "Hello World" to `String` variables. The program calculates and displays the following information:

   - Length of the two strings
   - Index of the first character 'o'
   - Index of the next character 'o'
   - Concatenation of the variable containing "Hi" with a substring of the variable containing "Hello World"; the substring begins at the position of the space immediately preceding the character 'W' and extends through the end of the string
   - The second `String` variable in all lowercase characters
   - The second `String` variable in all uppercase characters

   Write your design in the following space. Your design should be a list of Java comments without any code.

1. b. Write a Java program ba   on the design you created in Exercise 1a. Enter the program, saving it as **Words.java**, and   en execute the program. Copy the output and save it according to your instructor's requirem   ts. Text output can be saved in a block comment at the end of your program. Save your s   rce code to the device or location specified by your instructor.

Following is a copy of the   een results that should appear.

```
This program demonst    es commonly used string methods.

The output displayed    s the string values "Hi" and "Hello World"

The length of the str    "Hello World" is 11
The index of the firs    aracter 'o' in "Hello World" is 4
The index of the seco    haracter 'o' in "Hello World" is 7
The concatenation of    and " World" is "Hi World"
The string value "Hell    ld" in all lowercase is hello world
The string value "Hell    ld" in all uppercase is HELLO WORLD
```

LAB 3.3 FORMATTING NUMERIC DATA, PARSING NUMERIC STRINGS, AND USING DIALOG BOXES FOR INPUT AND OUTPUT

In previous chapters and assignments, you displayed data to the standard output stream using the methods `print` and `println`. Programmers have little control over the format of output produced by these methods, though. For example, let's say you have a numeric variable that contains price information, such as the following:

```
double price = 47.50;
```

In the United States, currency amounts usually are displayed with exactly two digits to the right of the decimal point. Unfortunately, a `print` or `println` statement such as this one:

```
System.out.println("The price is $" + price);
```

produces results that are not formatted as we would like:

```
The price is $47.5
```

The predefined method `printf` gives you the ability to more precisely control output formatting. The first argument of `printf` is a *format string* made up of text and *format specifiers*, which tell Java exactly how to format printed values. Following the format string are the values to be printed using the format specifiers in the format string. For example, let's modify the earlier example to print both quantity and price:

```
int quantity = 10;
double price = 47.50;
System.out.printf("The price for %d items is $%.2f%n",
    quantity, price);
```

The format string in this `printf` call specifies that quantity will be printed as a decimal integer ("`%d`"), price will be printed as a floating-point value with exactly two digits after its decimal point ("`%.2f`"), and output is terminated with a newline character ("`%n`"). These statements produce the following output:

```
The price for 10 items is $47.50
```

In addition to input methods such as `nextInt`, `nextDouble`, and `next`, and output methods such as `print`, `println`, and `printf`, Java provides support for input and output using its *graphical user interface (GUI)*. This can be accomplished using the two methods `showInputDialog` (for input) and `showMessageDialog` (for output) of the `JOptionPane` class. `JOptionPane` is contained in the package `javax.swing`, so GUI applications usually import this class or its entire package. GUI applications also must include the statement:

```
System.exit(0);
```

to ensure they terminate properly.

The `showInputDialog` method has a string parameter, and it opens a *dialog box* using the parameter to prompt the user to enter a value. The dialog box contains a *text field* into which the user can enter a string, and two buttons labeled *OK* and *Cancel*. The method returns the value entered into the text box if the user clicks the *OK* button or presses the *Enter key*. If the user clicks the *Cancel* button, the method returns the predefined value `null`.

The `showMessageDialog` method requires four parameters: the *parent component* of the dialog box, the *message text* to be displayed in the dialog box, the *box title* to be displayed in the *title bar* of the dialog box, and the *message type* that determines what—if any—icon will be displayed alongside the message text. The method opens a dialog box, the appearance of which is dictated by the four parameters. The dialog box also contains an *OK* button that the user can click to make the dialog box disappear. The parent component parameter is an object that represents the parent window of the dialog box. If `null` is used as the value of the parent component argument, the dialog box appears in the middle of the screen.

The value entered by the user and returned by the method `showInputDialog` is a string value. If the string represents a numeric value, then it must be *parsed* (converted to an actual numeric value) before you can perform arithmetic operations on it. Java provides methods in predefined classes known as *wrapper classes* that accommodate these conversions. These methods include:

- `Integer.parseInt(strExpression)` – Convert to an `int` value

- `Double.parseDouble(strExpression)` – Convert to a `double` value

Earlier, we saw how `printf` can be used to format displayed values precisely. But the formatted results of `printf` can only be displayed, not stored in a `String` variable. To address this need, Java provides `format`, a method of the `String` class; `format` has the same parameters as `printf` but returns its results as a string value rather than printing them. Using `format`, you can build nicely formatted strings for use with the method `showMessageDialog`.

Objectives

In this lab, you become acquainted with using the dialog box for input and output, parsing input data, and formatting the output of numbers.

After completing this lab, you will be able to:

- Input data through the dialog box.

- Output messages through the dialog box.

- Parse input data from the keyboard.

- Parse input data from the dialog box.

- Format the output of decimal numbers.

> Estimated completion time: **40–60 minutes**

Formatting Numeric Data, Parsing Numeric Strings, and Using Dialog Boxes for Input and Output

Write complete Java programs from the instructions and output examples given.

1. a. *Critical Thinking Exercise*: Redesign the program **Realtor.java**, which you created in Chapter 2 and saved to the device or location specified by your instructor.

Use a dialog box to ask the user to enter the last name of the homeowner. Use another dialog box to ask the user to enter the selling price of the home. Use a third dialog box to display a message with the owner's name, the selling price of the home, the cost to the owner to sell the home, and the amount of the commission the selling agent will receive. Format the decimal output showing two decimal places.

Write your design in the following space. Your design should be a list of Java comments without any code.

1. b.   Write a Java program based on the design you created in Exercise 1a. Enter the program, saving it as **Home1.java**, and then execute the program. Follow your instructor's requirements for submitting output. Save your source code and your .class file to the device or location specified by your instructor.

(Windows users can copy the active window or dialog box by pressing *Alt+Print Scrn* to copy the active window or dialog box to the Clipboard. Each time a new dialog box appears during execution, you can save the output to a separate document using a program such as Microsoft Word. If this is done, name your document **Home1Screens.doc**, and then print the Home1Screens document and attach it to a printed copy of your program.)

(UNIX users should save their .class file to disk, then either submit the disk or send the file electronically to their instructor.)

Following are copies of dialog boxes that should appear as your program executes. The exact appearance depends on the data entered.

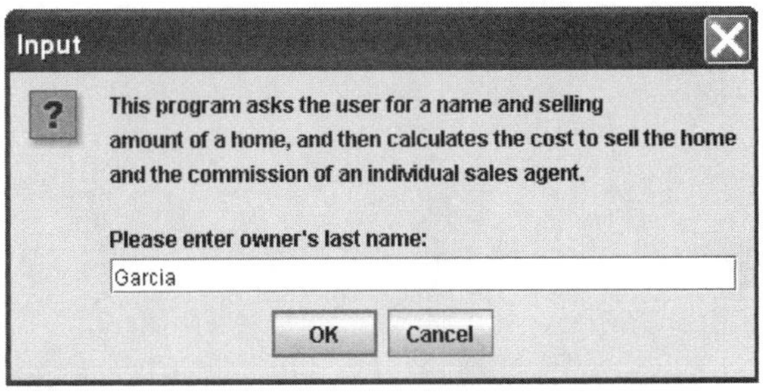

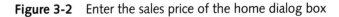

Figure 3-1   Enter owner's name dialog box

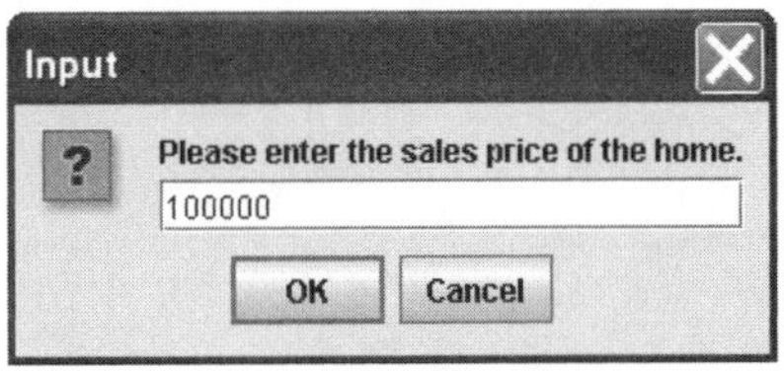

Figure 3-2   Enter the sales price of the home dialog box

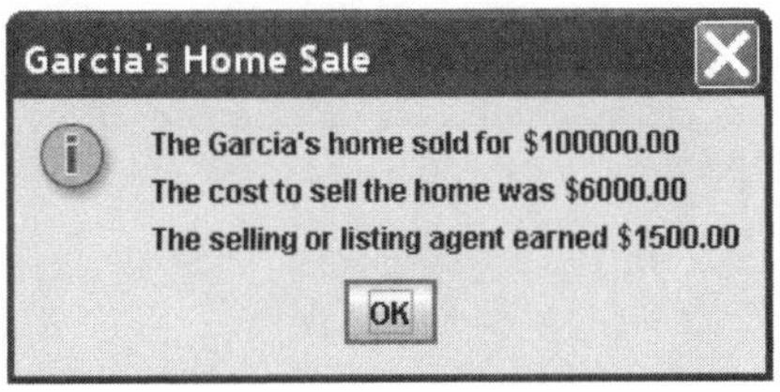

Figure 3-3   Garcia's Home Sale dialog box

2. a.   Redesign the program **Home1.java** you created and saved earlier in this chapter so that it does not use GUI input and output. Prompt the user to input the homeowner name and selling price on one line, separated by a space. Read the name and price into separate **String** variables. Parse the selling price to a **double** variable. Perform all output using **printf**, displaying the numeric values with two decimal places.

Write your design in the following space. Your design should be a list of Java comments without any code.

2. b.   Write a Java program based on the design you created in Exercise 2a. Enter the program, saving it as **Home2.java**, and then execute the program. Follow your instructor's requirements for submitting output. Save your source code and your .class file to the device or location specified by your instructor.

(Windows users can select, copy, and paste text output into a block comment at the end of their program. UNIX users should save their .class file to disk, then either submit the disk or send the file electronically to their instructor.)

Your instructor might prefer that you submit the .class file electronically with your program. Save your source code and your .class file to the device or location specified by your instructor.

Following is a copy of screen results that might appear depending on the data entered. The input entered by the user appears in bold.

```
This program asks the user for a name and selling
amount of a home, and then calculates the cost to sell the home
and the commission of an individual sales agent.

Please enter owner's last name and the sales price of the home:
Garcia 100000
The Garcia's home sold for $100000.00
The cost to sell the home was $6000.00
The selling or listing agent earned $1500.00
```

LAB 3.4 USING FILES FOR INPUT AND OUTPUT

Inputting data from the keyboard and displaying the output to the screen is convenient when you are working with a small amount of data. For large amounts of data, this method is inefficient. In addition, you might want to check input for accuracy before processing it, and save output for later uses. Data can be read from and written to a data file. A *file* is a named area in secondary storage used to hold information. Java provides three classes that can be used for file input and output: `FileReader` is an input class, and `FileWriter` and `PrintWriter` are output classes. All three of these classes are contained in the package `java.io`, so you usually include an import statement to use them.

In earlier programs, you read input from the keyboard using an object of the `Scanner` class that was created with the standard input stream, `System.in`. To input data from a file using the same methods you use to input data from the keyboard, you create an object of the class `FileReader`, and then use it to create a `Scanner` object. To send output to a file using the same methods you use to output data to `System.out`, you create and use an object of the class `PrintWriter`.

When creating a `FileReader` or `PrintWriter` object, you associate it with the name and location of an input or output file, respectively. This is known as *opening* the file. The format of the location is system-dependent. For example, on a Microsoft Windows system, the file named "pgm.txt" located in the top-level folder of the system drive is specified as "c:\pgm.txt". On a UNIX system, the file named "pgm.txt" located within the subdirectory "apc" of the directory "usr" is specified as "/usr/apc/pgm.txt".

An input file must exist before it can be opened. If it does not, then the statement that opens the file fails and throws a `FileNotFoundException` exception. An output file does not have to exist before it is opened. If it does exist, by default, the old contents are erased when the file is opened.

Output files should be closed using the method `close` when they are completed. This ensures that the contents of the output buffer are written to the file before the program terminates. Input files also can be closed when you have finished using them.

Objectives

In this lab, you use files for input and output.

After completing this lab, you will be able to:

- Associate file variables with I/O sources.
- Open and close input and output files.
- Read data from input files.
- Write data to output files.
- Work with multiple data files.

Estimated completion time: **50–60 minutes**

Using Files for Input and Output

Write complete Java programs from the instructions and output examples given.

1. a. *Critical Thinking Exercise*: Design a Java program that a small gift shop could use to order merchandise. The wholesaler requires that you send your order as a file over the Internet. Create your order file by entering your input through dialog boxes and writing to an output file named **order.out**. The order information that is output for each item consists of two lines: The first line contains the quantity of the item, a blank, the wholesale cost for that quantity of

items, and an end-of-line character. The second line contains the description of the item and an end-of-line character. Design your program to ask for two different items to order.

Write your design in the following space. Your design should be a list of Java comments without any code.

1. b. Write a Java program based on the design you created in Exercise 1a. Enter the program, saving it as **Gifts1.java**, and then execute the program. Follow your instructor's requirements for submitting output. Save your source code, your .class file, and your **order.out** file to the device or location specified by your instructor.

(Windows users can copy the active window or dialog box by pressing *Alt+Print Scrn* to copy the active window or dialog box to the Clipboard. Each time a new dialog box appears during execution, you can save the output to a separate document using a program such as Microsoft Word. If this is done, name your document **Gifts1Screens.doc**, and then print the Gifts1Screens document and attach it to a printed copy of your program along with the printed copy of your **order.out** file.)

(UNIX users should save their .class file to disk, then either submit the disk or send the file electronically to their instructor.)

Following are copies of dialog boxes that might appear depending on the data entered. After the dialog boxes, a copy of the **order.out** file that you created is displayed.

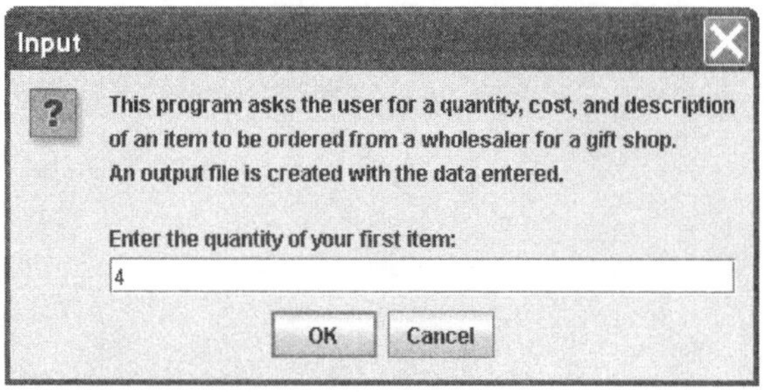

Figure 3-4   Program description and enter quantity dialog box

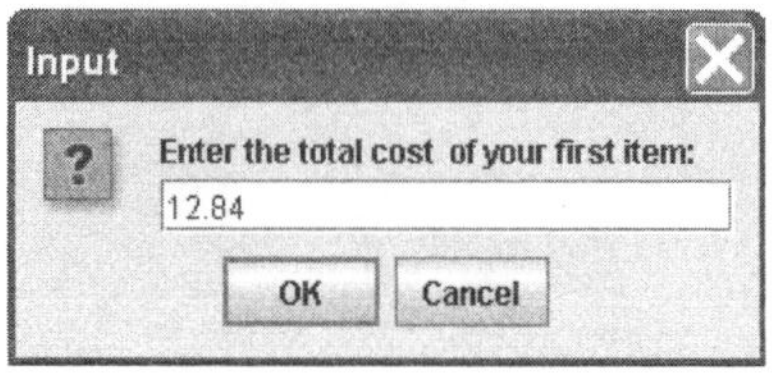

Figure 3-5   Enter cost dialog box

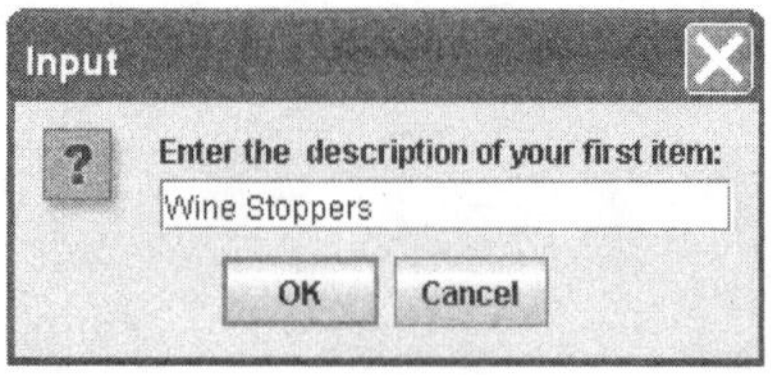

Figure 3-6   Enter description dialog box

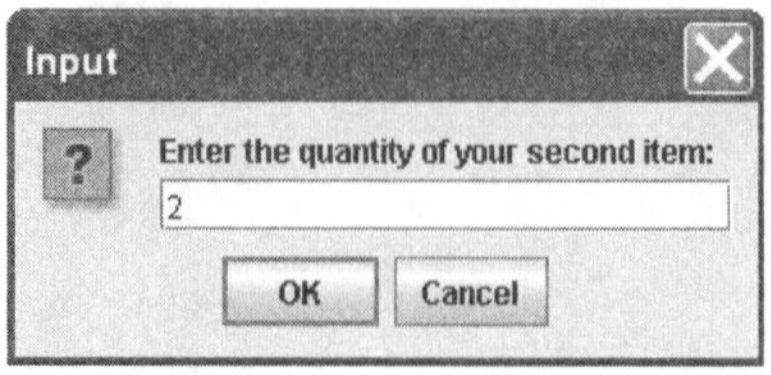

Figure 3-7   Enter second quantity dialog box

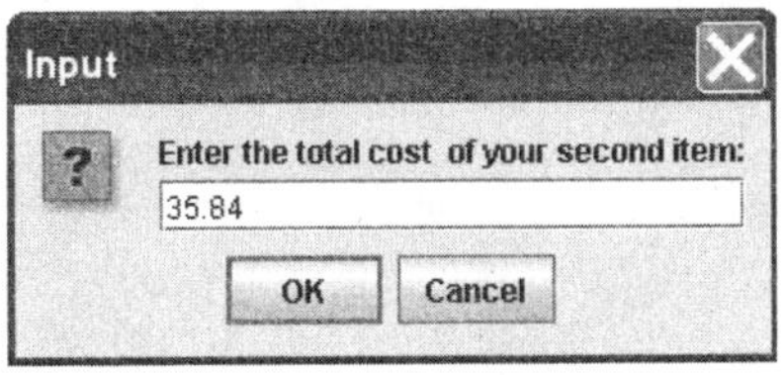

Figure 3-8   Enter second cost dialog box

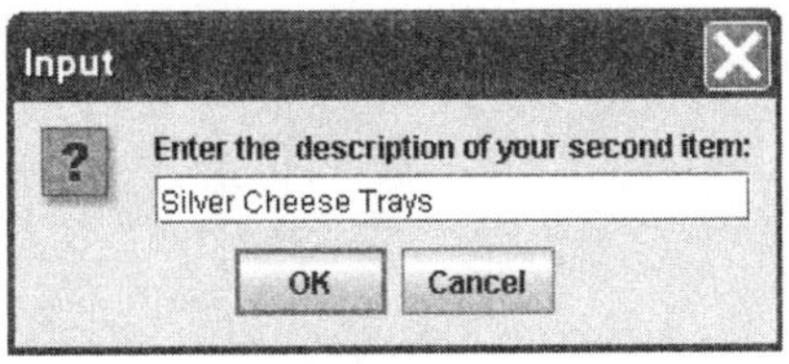

Figure 3-9   Enter second description dialog box

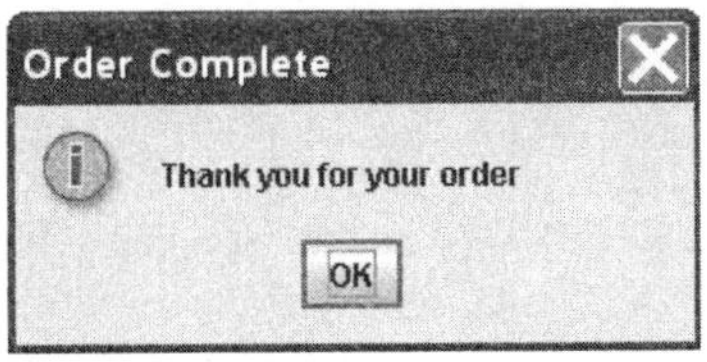

Figure 3-10   Thank you dialog box

Order.out data file

```
4 12.84
Wine Stoppers
2 35.64
Silver Cheese Trays
```

2. a. Design a program that builds on **Gifts1.java**. Copy the **order.out** file that you created in Lab 3.4 Exercise 1 and save it as **order.in** to the device or location specified by your instructor.

After the gift shop has received an order from the wholesaler, the program should create an inventory file. Assume that all items ordered were received. Design your program to read the file **order.in** and write the file **inventory.out**. The file **inventory.out** will contain the number of items received, the retail cost that is found by dividing the wholesale cost by the quantity ordered and multiplying by 2.4, and the description of the item.

Write your design in the following space. Your design should be a list of Java comments without any code.

2. b. Write a Java program based on the design you created in Exercise 2a. Enter the program, saving it as **Gifts2.java**, and then execute the program. Follow your instructor's requirements for submitting output. Save your source code, your .class file, and your **inventory.out** file to the device or location specified by your instructor.

(Windows users can copy the active window or dialog box by pressing *Alt+Print Scrn* to copy the active window or dialog box to the Clipboard. Each time a new dialog box appears during execution, you can save the output to a separate document using a program such as Microsoft Word. If this is done, name your document **Gifts2Screens.doc**, and then print the Gifts2Screens document and attach it to a printed copy of your program along with the printed copy of your **inventory.out** file.)

(UNIX users should save their .class file to disk, then either submit the disk or send the file electronically to their instructor.)

Following are copies of dialog boxes that might appear depending on the data in the file **order.in**. After the dialog boxes is a copy of the **inventory.out** file.

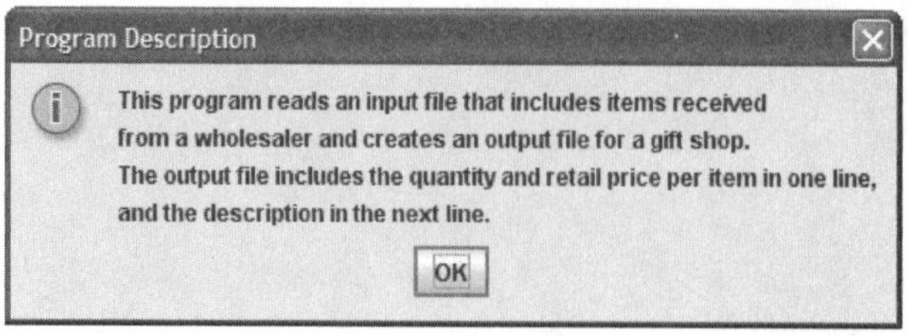

Figure 3-11   Inventory program description dialog box

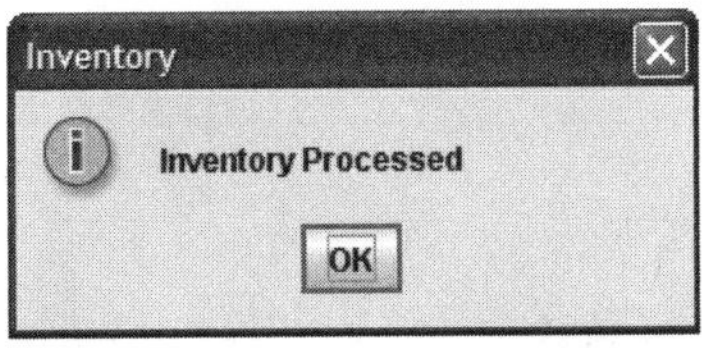

Figure 3-12   Inventory Processed dialog box

Inventory.out data file

```
4 7.70
Wine Stopper
2 42.77
Silver Cheese Tray
```

CHAPTER

4

CONTROL STRUCTURES I: SELECTION

In this chapter, you will:

♦ Learn about control structures

♦ Examine relational and logical operators

♦ Explore how to form and evaluate logical (Boolean) expressions

♦ Discover how to use the selection control structures `if`, `if...else`, and `switch` in a program

CHAPTER 4: ASSIGNMENT COVER SHEET

Name _____   Date _____

Section _____

Lab Assignments	Grade
Lab 4.1 Using Relational and Logical Operators to Evaluate Logical (Boolean) Expressions	
Lab 4.2 Using the Selection Control Structures `if` and `if...else`	
Lab 4.3 Using Nested `if` and `if...else` Statements	
Lab 4.4 Using the Conditional Operator (`?:`)	
Lab 4.5 Using the `switch` Selection Control Structure (Critical Thinking Exercises)	
Total Grade	

See your instructor or the introduction to this book for instructions on submitting your assignments.

```
3. if (x < 8)
   {
       System.out.println("x is within the range.\n");
       System.out.println("This is a true statement.\n");
   }
   System.out.println("And, after selection, the next statement is
   executed.\n");
```

```
4. if (x == 6 || found)
         System.out.println("Problem 4 is true.\n");
   System.out.println("End of Problem 4\n");
```

```
5. if (x == 6 && found)
        System.out.println("Problem 5 is true.\n");
   System.out.println("End of Problem 5\n");
```

```
6. if (x !=6 && !found)
         System.out.println("Problem 6 is true.\n");
   System.out.println("End of Problem 6\n");
```

```
7. if (x > 0 && x < 10)
        System.out.println("x is in range\n");
   System.out.println("The value of x is " + x + ".\n");
```

8.
```java
if (x > 10)
      System.out.println("x is greater than 10.\n");
   else
      System.out.println( "x is less than or equal to 10.\n");
   System.out.println( "Selection allows decision making.\n");
```

9.
```java
if (x == 6)
      System.out.println( "A match is found.\n");
   else
      System.out.println( "A match was not found.\n");
   System.out.println( "Sequence continues after selection is complete.\n");
```

10.
```java
if (!(x < 8))
   {
         System.out.println("x is within the range.\n");
         System.out.println("This is a true statement.\n");
   }
   else
   {
         System.out.println("x is out of range.\n");
         System.out.println("This is a false statement.\n");
   }
   System.out.println("After selection, the next statement is executed.\n");
```

11.
```java
if (x >= 5)
   {
   }
   else
      System.out.println( "Have a good day.\n");
   System.out.println( "The value of x is " + x + '\n');
```

```
1.  f (x == 6 && found)
        System.out.println( "Problem 5 is true.\n");
    e.
    {
            stem.out.println( "Problem 5 is false.\n");
         S  em.out.println( "Both conditions must be true.\n");
    }
    System.   .println("End of Problem 5\n");
```

```
13. if (x !=6 && !t   d)
        System.out.p  tln( "Problem 6 is true.\n");
    else
        System.out.pri   n( "Problem 6 is false.\n");
    System.out.println(   d of Problem 6\n");
```

```
14. if (x > 0 && x < 10)
        System.out.println( "x i   range\n");
    else
        System.out.println( "x is    in range\n");
```

LAB 4.3 USING NESTED if AND if...else STATEMENTS

The statement(s) executed in a selection can be any valid Java statement. This includes an `if` statement located within another `if` or `if...else` statement. These statements are called *nested if* statements. When the selection requires more than two alternatives, use a nested `if` statement.

An `else` statement is not required when using an `if` statement; however, when used, each `else` statement must be paired with an `if`. In a nested `if` statement, Java associates an `else` with the most recent incomplete `if`—that is, the most recent `if` that has not been paired with an `else`.

An alternative to writing nested `if...else` statements is to write compound Boolean expressions.

Objectives

In this lab, you evaluate Boolean expressions in nested `if` statements.

After completing this lab, you will be able to:

- Match the `else` statement with the appropriate `if` statement.

- Know when to nest and when not to nest `if` statements.

- Write code using nested `if`s.

- Write compound Boolean expressions using `if...else` statements.

Estimated completion time: **40–50 minutes**

Using Nested if and if...else Statements

Determine the results of executing the following Java statements. To do so, step through the statements, and then write what should be displayed.

```
1. int temperature = 78;
   int month = 6;
   String name = "Pat Boone";
   if (temperature >= 70 && month >=6)
       System.out.println("Wear sandals\n");
   else if (name == "Pat Boone")
       System.out.println("Wear white shoes\n");
   else
       System.out.println("Wear black shoes\n");
```

2. a. What is the output of the program when temperature = 70, month = 5, and name = "Pat Boone"?

2. b. What is the output of the program when temperature = 60, month = 5, and name = "Pat Boone"?

2. c. What is the output of the program when temperature = 60, month = 5, and name = "Your name"?

3. a. Design a Java program that asks the user for three names. Using compound and nested `if` statements, display the names in alphabetical order. Write your design in the following space. Your design should be a list of Java comments without any code.

3. b. Write a Java program based on the design you created in Exercise 3a. Enter the program, saving it as **NameSort.java** to the device or location specified by your instructor. Then execute the program four times, entering the names in a different order each time.

■ Enter the names Oswald, Anne, and Jorge separated by spaces with no commas.

■ Enter the names Oswald, Jorge, and Anne separated by spaces with no commas.

■ Enter the names Anne, Oswald, and Jorge separated by spaces with no commas.

■ Enter the names Jorge, Anne, and Oswald separated by spaces with no commas.

As your program executes, print the screen each time a new dialog box appears and paste the output in a document, such as a Microsoft Word or WordPad document. (In Windows, press *Alt+Print Scrn* to copy the active window or dialog box to the Clipboard. Then open a document and press *Ctrl+V* to paste the screen.) Name your document **NameSortScreens.doc**. Print the NameSortScreens document and attach it to a printed copy of your program. Save your source code and screen document to the device or location specified by your instructor.

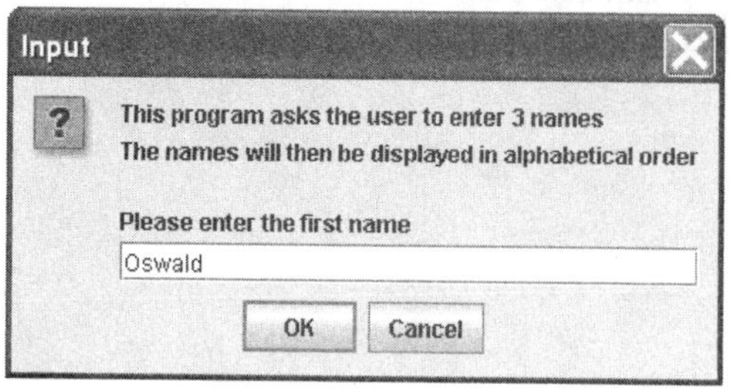

Figure 4-1   Enter first name dialog box for first test

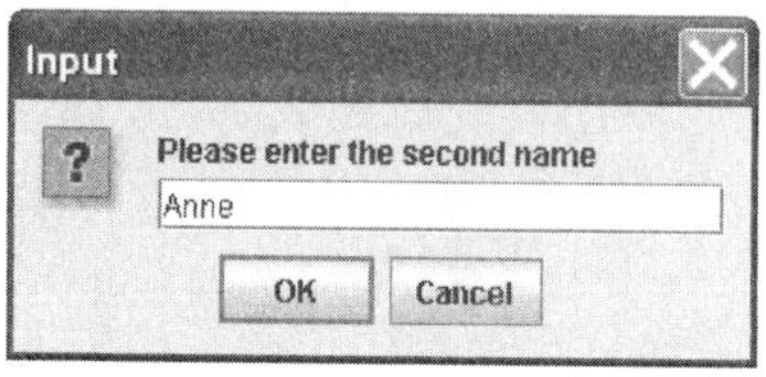

Figure 4-2   Enter second name dialog box for first test

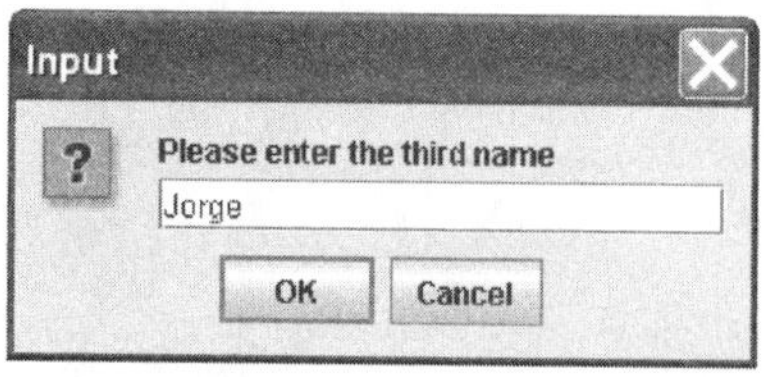

Figure 4-3   Enter third name dialog box for first test

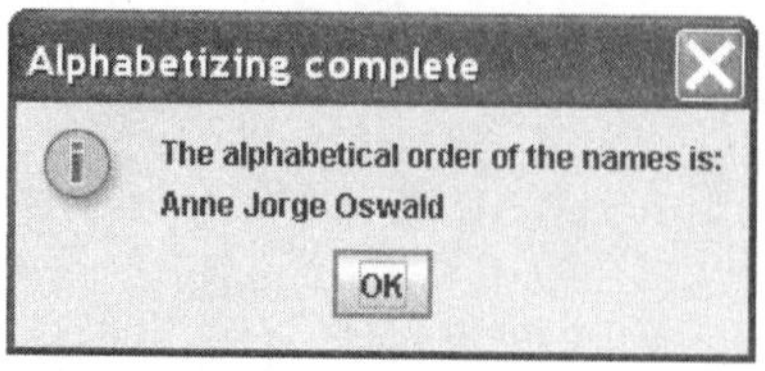

Figure 4-4   Alphabetizing complete dialog box for first test

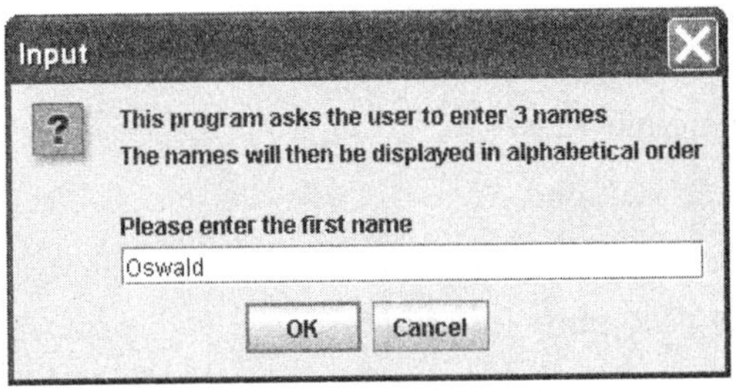

Figure 4-5   Enter first name dialog box for second test

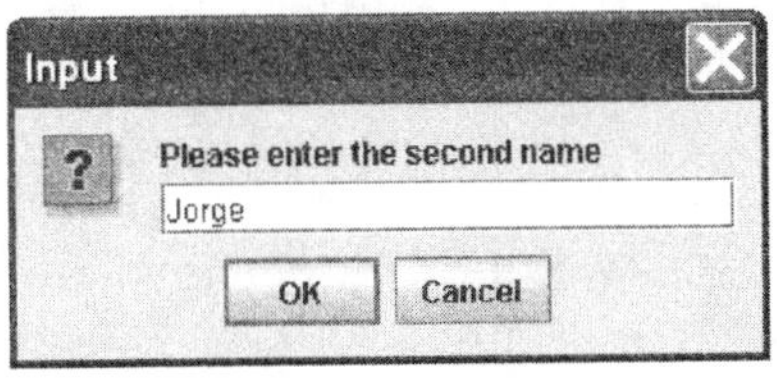

Figure 4-6   Enter second name dialog box for second test

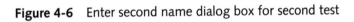

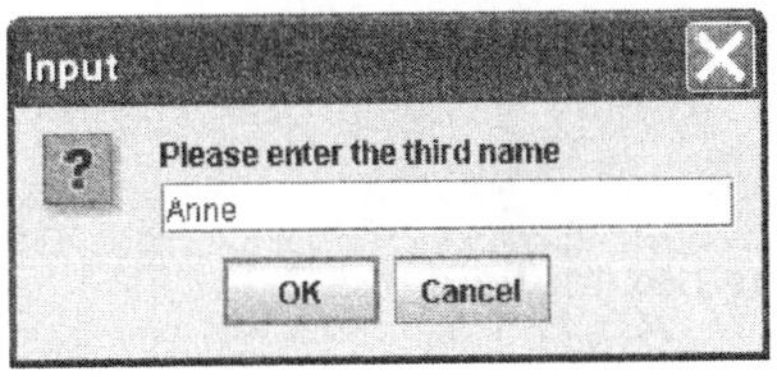

Figure 4-7   Enter third name dialog box for second test

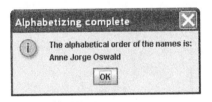

Figure 4-8   Alphabetizing complete dialog box for second test

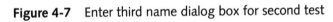

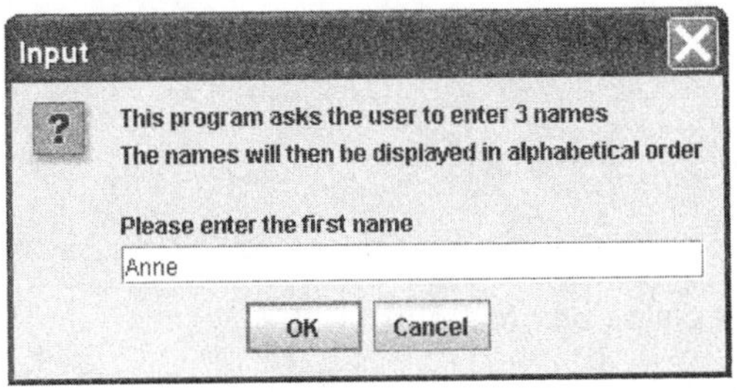

Figure 4-9   Enter first name dialog box for third test

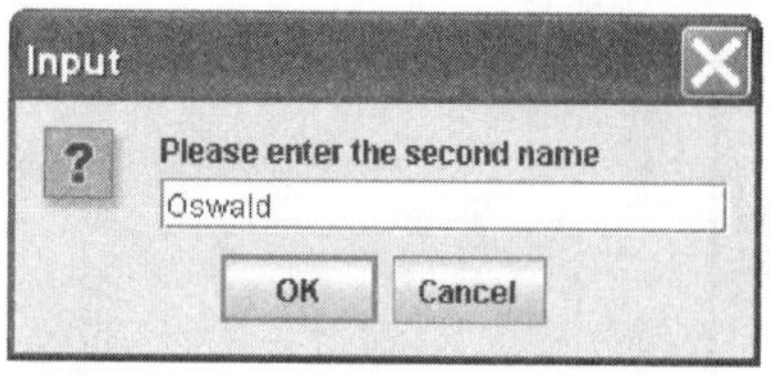

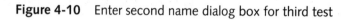

Figure 4-10   Enter second name dialog box for third test

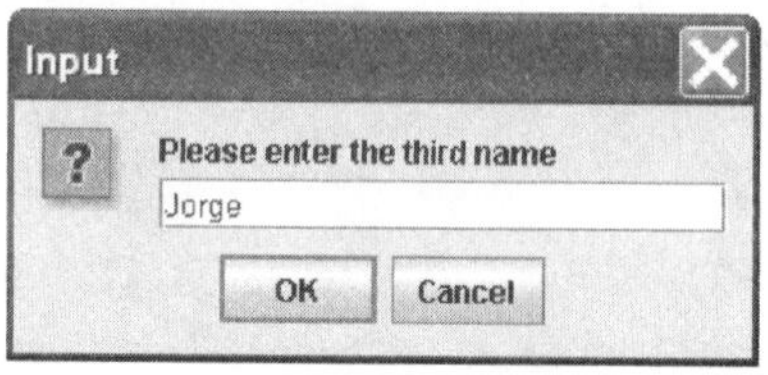

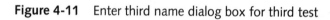

Figure 4-11   Enter third name dialog box for third test

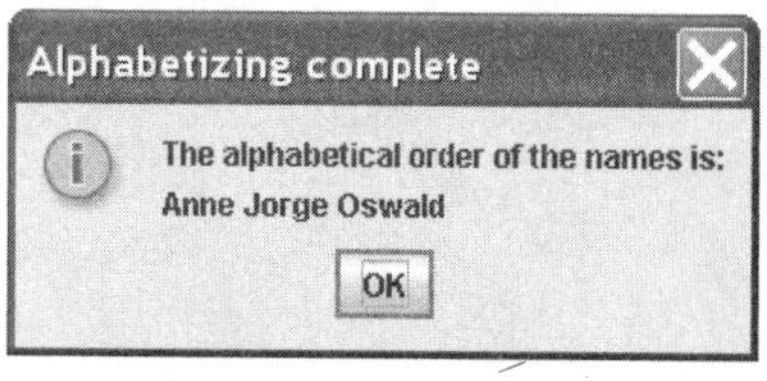

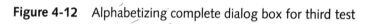

Figure 4-12   Alphabetizing complete dialog box for third test

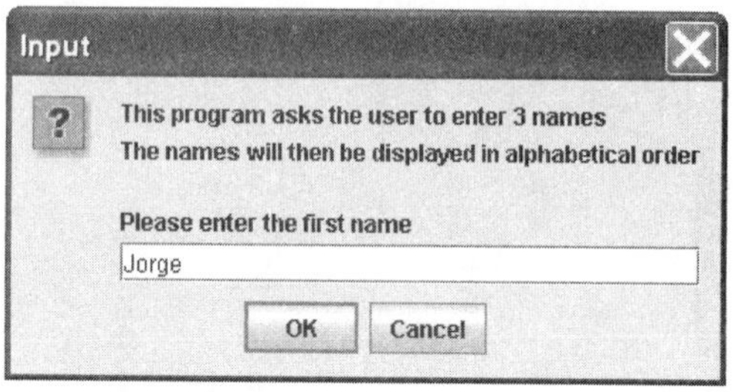

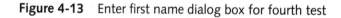

Figure 4-13   Enter first name dialog box for fourth test

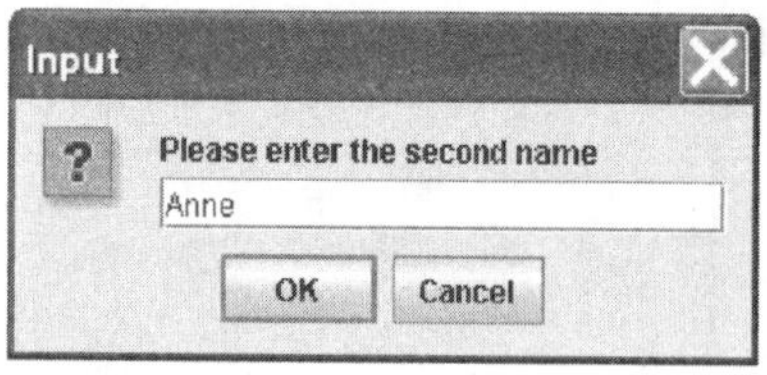

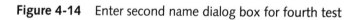

Figure 4-14   Enter second name dialog box for fourth test

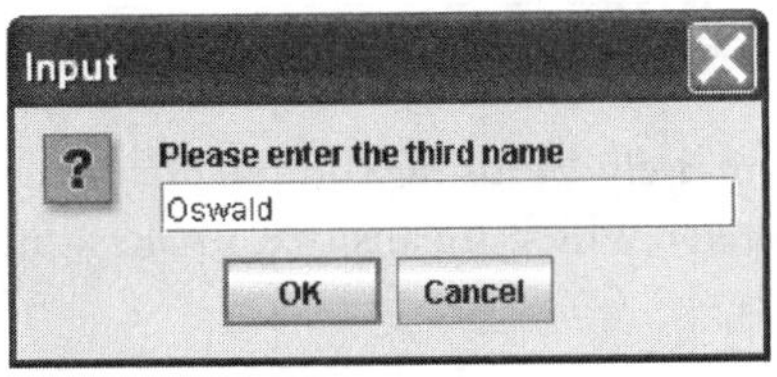

Figure 4-15   Enter third name dialog box for fourth test

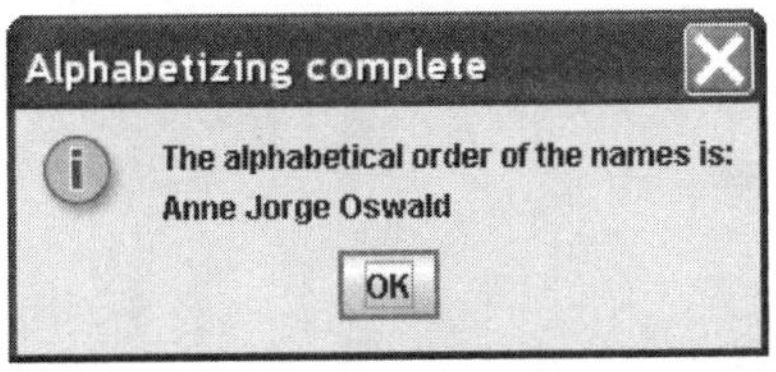

Figure 4-16   Alphabetizing complete dialog box for fourth test

LAB 4.4 USING THE CONDITIONAL OPERATOR (?:)

You can write certain if...else statements concisely by using the *conditional operator* in Java. The conditional operator, written as ?:, is a *ternary operator*, which means that it takes three arguments. The general syntax for the conditional operator follows:

```
(expression1) ? expression2 : expression3
```

For example, consider the following code.

```
int x = 10, sum = 0;
if(x == 10)
    sum = x + 3;
else
    sum = x - 3;
```

You can write these statements using the conditional operator:

```
int x = 10, sum = 0;
sum = (x == 10) ? x + 3 : x - 3;
```

In these examples, sum is assigned 13 because x is equal to 10.

Notice that this code does not use the reserved word if.

An expression that uses the conditional operator is called a *conditional expression*, and it is evaluated as follows: If expression1 evaluates to true, the result of the conditional expression is expression2. Otherwise, the result of the conditional expression is expression3.

Objectives

In this lab, you rewrite if...else statements using the conditional operator.

After completing this lab, you will be able to:

- Write if...else statements using the conditional operator.

Estimated completion time: **10–15 minutes**

Using the Conditional Operator (?:)

Rewrite the following if...else statements using the conditional operator:

```
1. double value = 8.9;
   if (value > 10.6)
       System.out.println("x is greater than 10.\n");
   else
       System.out.println("x is less than or equal to 10.\n");
```

```
2. int x = 4;
      if (x == 6)
          System.out.println("A match is found.\n");
      else
          System.out.println("A match was not found.\n");
```

LAB 4.5 USING THE switch SELECTION CONTROL STRUCTURE

The third control structure, called the switch statement, gives the program the power to choose from among many alternatives.

A switch structure evaluates an expression, and then uses the value of the expression to perform the actions specified in the statements that follow the reserved word case. The value of the expression must be integral and is sometimes called the *selector*. An integral value is a value that evaluates to an integer value.

The syntax of the switch statement is as follows:

```
switch (expression)
{
case value1:
   statements1
   break;
case value2:
   statements2
   break;
   ...
case valuen:
   statementsn
   break;
default:
   statements
}
```

The switch statement executes according to the following rules:

- When the value of the expression matches a case value, the statements execute until either a break statement is found or the end of the switch structure is reached. Execution of a break statement exits the switch statement immediately.

- If the value of the expression matches no case value, the statements following the default label execute. If there is no match and no default label, the entire switch statement is skipped.

The switch statement is an elegant way to implement multiple selections. If multiple selections involve a range of values, you should convert each range to a finite set of values. For instance, if all values 60 to 69 are the range of values, you could divide by 10, and then use the 6 as the finite value.

Objectives

In this lab, you convert a nested if...else statement to a switch statement.

After completing this lab, you will be able to:

- Write switch control statements using the break statement.

- Write switch control statements using the fall-through capability.

Estimated completion time: **30–40 minutes**

Using the switch Selection Control Structure

Write programs that use the switch statement, and then test them with different values.

1. a. *Critical Thinking Exercise*: Design a Java program that uses the switch statement and asks the user to select one of three television models. The program should provide a description of the models. Using the fall-through capability of the switch statement, display the model chosen, the description, and the price. The user should make a selection by model number:

   - Model 100 comes with remote control, timer, and stereo sound and costs $1000.

   - Model 200 comes with all features of model 100, plus picture-in-picture; it costs $1200.

   - Model 300 comes with all features of model 200 plus HDTV, flat screen, and 16 × 9 aspect ratio; it costs $2400.

   Use the following description and prompt for the program:

   ```
   This program asks the user to enter a television model number.
   The description of the model chosen will be displayed.

   Please enter the model number chosen
   Model 100 comes with remote control, timer
   and stereo sound and costs $1000
   Model 200 comes with all features of model 100
   and picture-in-picture, and costs $1200
   Model 300 comes with all features of model 200 and
   HDTV, flat screen, 16 x 9 aspect ratio and costs $2400
   ```

   Write your design in the following space. Your design should be a list of Java comments without any code.

1. b. Write a Java program based on the design you created in Exercise 1a. Enter the program, saving it as **TVmodel.java** to the device or location specified by your instructor. Execute the program three times, selecting a different model with each execution. As your program executes, print the screen each time a new dialog box appears and paste the output in a document, such as a Microsoft Word or WordPad document. (In Windows, press *Alt+Print Scrn* to copy the active window or dialog box to the Clipboard. Then open a document and press *Ctrl+V* to paste the screen.) Name your document **TVmodelScreens.doc**. Print the TVmodelScreens document and attach it to a printed copy of your program. Save your source code and screen document to the device or location specified by your instructor.

Following are copies of dialog boxes that should appear.

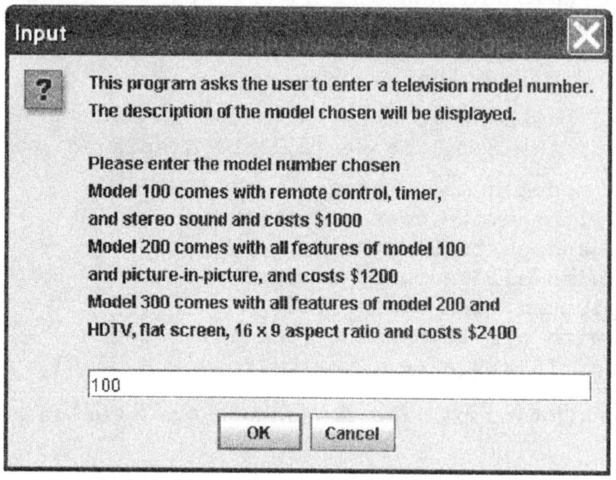

Figure 4-17 Selecting a television model dialog box for first test

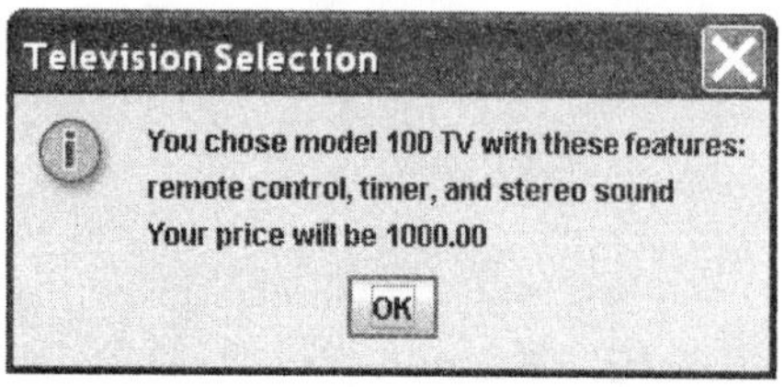

Figure 4-18 Television Selection dialog box for first test

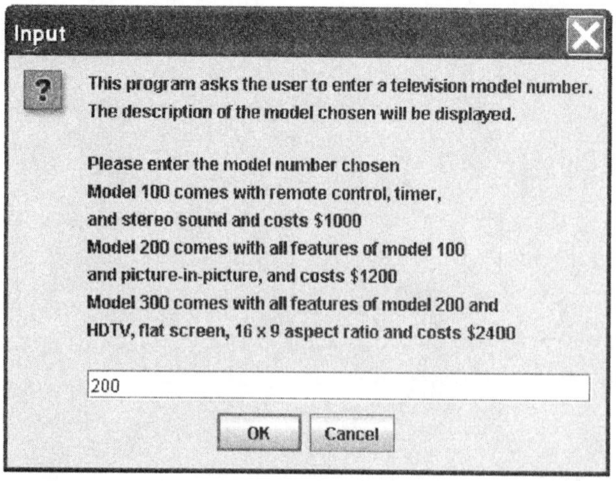

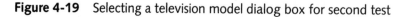

Figure 4-19 Selecting a television model dialog box for second test

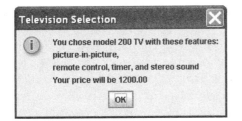

Television Selection

ⓘ You chose model 200 TV with these features:
picture-in-picture,
remote control, timer, and stereo sound
Your price will be 1200.00

OK

Figure 4-20   Television Selection dialog box for second test

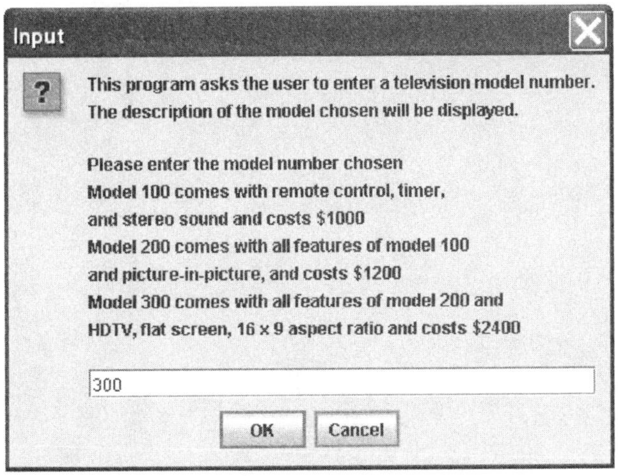

Input

❓ This program asks the user to enter a television model number.
The description of the model chosen will be displayed.

Please enter the model number chosen
Model 100 comes with remote control, timer,
and stereo sound and costs $1000
Model 200 comes with all features of model 100
and picture-in-picture, and costs $1200
Model 300 comes with all features of model 200 and
HDTV, flat screen, 16 x 9 aspect ratio and costs $2400

300

OK   Cancel

Figure 4-21   Selecting a television model dialog box for third test

Television Selection

ⓘ You chose model 300 TV with these features:
HDTV, flat screen, 16 x 9 aspect ratio
picture-in-picture,
remote control, timer, and stereo sound
Your price will be 2400.00

OK

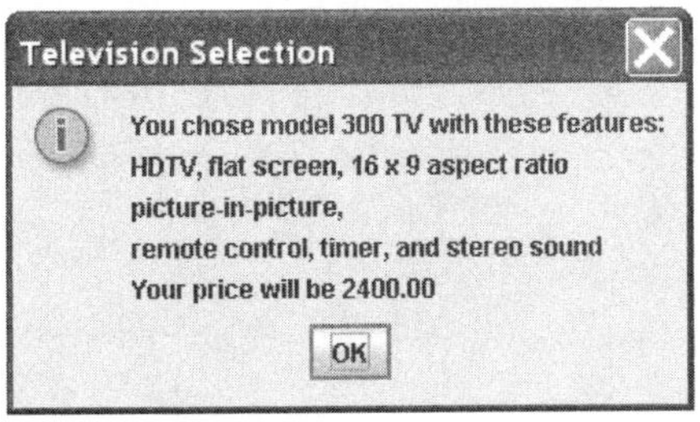

Figure 4-22   Television Selection dialog box for third test

2. a. *Critical Thinking Exercise*: Design a program for a builder that allows the user to select flooring options for building a home. The program should use an input dialog box to explain the purpose and use of the program, list flooring options, and ask the user to select one of the options by a numeric value. Use the `switch` statement. Display an information dialog box to display the selection made, the description, and the price. Use the following descriptions for the program:

```
This program asks the user to enter a choice
of flooring for a new home.
Enter the number that matches your flooring choice
1: Scored concrete, costs $3000
2: Carpeting comes with a $5000 allowance
3: Wood floors in the living area,
carpeting in the bedrooms, tile in the bath areas,
and a $5000 carpet allowance, totaling $10,000
```

Write your design in the following space. Your design should be a list of Java comments without any code.

2. b.   Write a Java program based on the design you created in Exercise 2a. Enter the program, saving it as **Flooring.java** to the device or location specified by your instructor. Then execute the program three times, selecting a different model with each execution. As your program executes, print the screen each time a new dialog box appears and paste the output in a document, such as a Microsoft Word or WordPad document. (In Windows, press *Alt+Print Scrn* to copy the active window or dialog box to the Clipboard. Then open a document and press *Ctrl+V* to paste the screen.) Name your document **FlooringScreens.doc**. Print the FlooringScreens document and attach it to a printed copy of your program. Save your source code and screen document to the device or location specified by your instructor.

Following are copies of dialog boxes that should appear.

Input

? This program asks the user to enter a choice of flooring for a new home.
Enter the number that matches your flooring choice
1: Scored concrete, costs $3000
2: Carpeting comes with a $5000 allowance
3: Wood floors in the living area,
carpeting in the bedrooms, tile in the bath areas,
and a $5000 carpet allowance, totaling $10,000

1

OK   Cancel

Figure 4-23   Select flooring dialog box for first test

Flooring Selection

(i) You chose selection 1 - Scored concrete, costs $3000

OK

Figure 4-24   Flooring Selection dialog box for first test

Flooring Selection

(i) You chose selection 2 - Carpeting comes with a $5000 allowance

OK

Figure 4-25   Flooring Selection dialog box for second test

Flooring Selection

(i) You chose selection 3 - Wood floors in the living area,
carpeting in the bedrooms, tile in the bath areas,
and a $5000 carpet allowance, totaling $10,000

OK

Figure 4-26   Flooring Selection dialog box for third test

5

CONTROL STRUCTURES II: REPETITION

In this chapter, you will:

♦ Learn about repetition (looping) control structures

♦ Explore how to construct and use count-controlled, sentinel-controlled, flag-controlled, and EOF-controlled repetition structures

♦ Examine `break` and `continue` statements

♦ Discover how to form and use nested control structures

CHAPTER 5: ASSIGNMENT COVER SHEET

Name _____　　Date _____

Section _____

Lab Assignments	Grade
Lab 5.1 Using the `while` Looping (Repetition) Structure	
Lab 5.2 Using the `for` Looping (Repetition) Structure	
Lab 5.3 Using the `do...while` Looping Repetition Structure (Critical Thinking Exercises)	
Lab 5.4 Using `break` and `continue` Statements	
Lab 5.5 Using Nested Control Structures (Critical Thinking Exercises)	
Total Grade	

See your instructor or the introduction to this book for instructions on submitting your assignments.

LAB 5.1 USING THE while LOOPING (REPETITION) STRUCTURE

The three looping (repetition) structures, while, for, and do...while, are reserved words in Java and are used when you want a program to execute a set of statements repeatedly. The three different types of looping structures offer flexibility in coding. This lab focuses on the while loop.

The reserved word while acts on a *loop condition*, which is a Boolean expression that serves as a decision maker for the loop. Generally, the work of the loop is accomplished within the *body* of the loop, which consists of a statement or a block of statements executed when the expression evaluates to true. The expression is reevaluated before each iteration of the body until the expression evaluates to false. If the condition never evaluates to false, an *infinite loop* will occur.

The loop condition for most while loops involves a *loop control variable*. The loop control variable must be initialized before reaching the loop, and its value must be updated at some time within the loop body so that the loop condition eventually becomes false.

If the loop condition is false the first time it is evaluated, the body of the loop is not executed.

Rarely, the expression itself accomplishes the entire work of the loop, and the loop has no body. This lab will not cover that situation.

There are four types of while loops: *counter-controlled, sentinel-controlled, flag-controlled,* and *EOF (end-of-file) controlled.*

Objectives

In this lab, you become acquainted with all four types of while loops.

After completing this lab, you will be able to:

- Write a counter-controlled while loop when you know exactly how many pieces of data need to be read.

- Write a sentinel-controlled while loop that uses a special sentinel value to end the loop.

- Write a flag-controlled while loop that uses a Boolean variable as a decision maker, and evaluates to false to end the loop.

- Write an EOF-controlled while loop that continues until the program reaches the end of the file.

Estimated completion time: **50–60 minutes**

Using the while Looping (Repetition) Structure

Design and write code for the Java programs that use while loops.

1. a.   Design a Java program that asks for the number of students registered in a course. The user should be prompted to enter the number of students enrolled in a course. If the number of students is greater than 0, use a counter-controlled while loop to prompt the user to enter the names of the students registered for the class. Create an output file that contains the names of the students in the class. Display a message to the user when the program is complete.

Following is a copy of the screen results that might appear after running your program, depending on the data entered. The input entered by the user is in bold.

```
This program asks the user to enter the
number and names of students in a course.

How many students are registered for this class? 10

Enter the student's name: George Smith
Enter the student's name: Elaine Sanders
Enter the student's name: Jack Cunningham
Enter the student's name: Susie Brown
Enter the student's name: Marvella Garcia
Enter the student's name: Tony Peterson
Enter the student's name: John Jones
Enter the student's name: Mary Evans
Enter the student's name: Nancy Drew
Enter the student's name: Lola Zapata

The class is full.
```

Write your design in the following space. Your design should be a list of Java comments without any code.

1. b.   Write a Java program based on the design you created in Exercise 1a. Enter your program and name it **Roster1.java**. Name your output file **student1.dat**.

Step through your code by hand and complete a memory chart showing what occurs in memory when the Java code is executed.

To fill out the memory chart for each variable, specify the name of the variable, its data type, the line number in which the variable is assigned its initial value, the initial value assigned to the variable, and the line numbers in which the variable's value changes. If all of the line numbers in which the variable's value changes will not fit on one memory chart line, use as many lines as needed to specify the line numbers.

Your answers will vary. The following memory chart shows an example of how a chart might start.

Variable name	Data type	Declaration line number	Initialization line number	Initial value	Change line number
limit	int	13	21	10	36

Execute your program. Then copy the output and save it in a block comment at the end of your program. Save your source code and output data file to the device or location specified by your instructor.

The output file should list student names. Print your output file and attach it to your work.

2. a. Design a program to simulate the order processing of a hardware store. To fill an order, workers place items on a conveyor belt to be grouped, billed, and shipped. Each item has a UPC code that designates the name of the item and its price. When an order is complete, a worker places a bar on the conveyor belt to separate the order from the next order. The bar has a UPC code of 999. The computer system scans the UPC code of each item and records its price. When the system reads the code on the bar, it creates a bill, which it writes to an output file for further processing later.

A specific value that designates the end of a sequence of input values is called a *sentinel value*. The UPC code of 999 is used as a sentinel value in this program.

The output file contains two lines for each product; the product name is on one line, and its price is on the next line. Prompt the user to scan the next item. When the system reads the value 999, display a message to the user indicating the number of items that have been scanned.

Following is a copy of the screen results that might appear after running your program, depending on the data entered. The input entered by the user is shown in bold.

```
This order-processing program simulates using a
code reader to scan an item and create an invoice.

Please scan the name of the first item: hammer
Please scan the price of the hammer: 9.95
Please scan the name of the next item: saw
Please scan the price of the saw: 20.15
Please scan the name of the next item: shovel
Please scan the price of the shovel: 35.40
Please scan the name of the next item: 999

3 items scanned.
```

Write your design in the following space. Your design should be a list of Java comments without any code.

2. b. Write a Java program based on the design you created in Exercise 2a. Enter your program and name it **Scan1.java**. Name your output file **invoice1.dat**.

After entering your code but before executing your program, step through your code by hand and complete a memory chart showing what occurs in memory when the Java code is executed.

To fill out the memory chart for each variable, specify the name of the variable, its data type, the line number in which the variable is assigned its initial value, the initial value assigned to the variable, and the line numbers in which the variable's value changes. If all of the line numbers in which the variable's value changes will not fit on one memory chart line, use as many lines as needed to specify the line numbers.

Variable name	Data type	Declaration line number	Initialization line number	Initial value	Change line number

Execute your program. Test your program with the following input:

```
hammer
9.95
saw
20.15
shovel
35.40
999
```

Copy the output and save it in a block comment at the end of your program. Save your source code and output data file to the device or location specified by your instructor. Print your output file and attach it to your work.

3. a. The file **invoice1.dat** created in Exercise 2 consists of a list of items with a description on one line followed by the price of the item on the next line. Design a program that prompts the user to enter an item. The item entered will be used to search a list in the **invoice1.dat** file until the program finds the item in the list or the end-of-file is reached. If the item is found, display the name and price of the item. If the item is not found, display the message that the item was not in the list. Format the price to show two decimal places. Use a flag-controlled `while` loop with a compound conditional expression that utilizes the Boolean variable `found` and the `Scanner` method `hasNext()`.

Figure 5-1 shows the screen results that might appear after running your program, depending on the data entered.

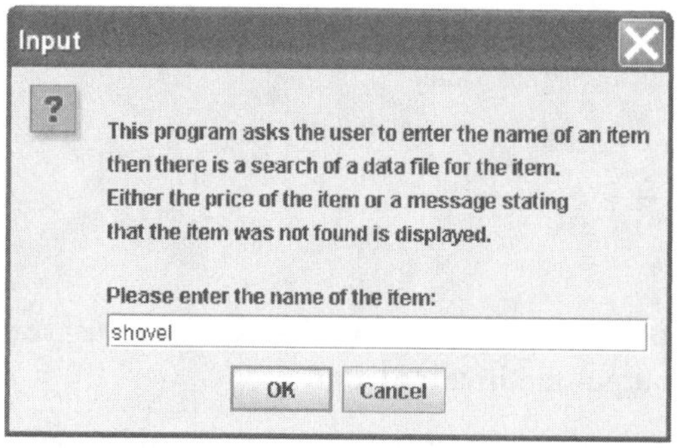

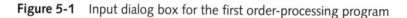

Figure 5-1   Input dialog box for the first order-processing program

Depending on the string entered and the data in the file, the output would resemble Figure 5-2.

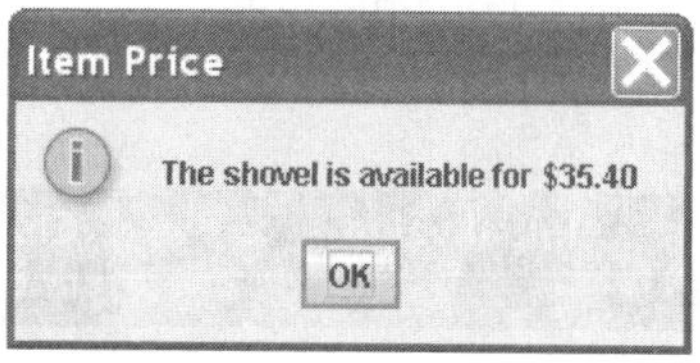

Figure 5-2   Item Price dialog box for the first order-processing program

Write your design in the following space. Your design should be a list of Java comments without any code.

3. b.   Write a Java program based on the design that you created in Exercise 3a. After entering your code but before executing your program, step through your code by hand and complete a memory chart showing what occurs in memory when the Java code is executed.

To fill out the memory chart for each variable, specify the name of the variable, its data type, the line number in which the variable is assigned its initial value, the initial value assigned to the variable, and the line numbers in which the variable's value changes. If all of the line numbers in which the variable's value changes will not fit on one memory chart line, use as many lines as needed to specify the line numbers.

Variable name	Data type	Declaration line number	Initialization line number	Initial value	Change line number

Save the program as **Find1.java** to the device or location specified by your instructor, and then compile, run, and test the program. Either copy the dialog boxes that appear and paste them into a document or print screens of the dialog boxes.

Test your program with the file **invoice1.dat** and with the following input:

```
shovel
```

Print your output file and program and attach them to your printed output screens to submit with your work.

4. a.   Consider the data file you created and processed in Exercises 2 and 3. Design a program that will read all of the data from the file **invoice1.dat** and total the price of all of the items. Because all data is read from a file, there are no prompts or input from the user. Display your data in currency format, with exactly two digits to the right of the decimal point.

Depending on the information in the file, the output should resemble Figure 5-3.

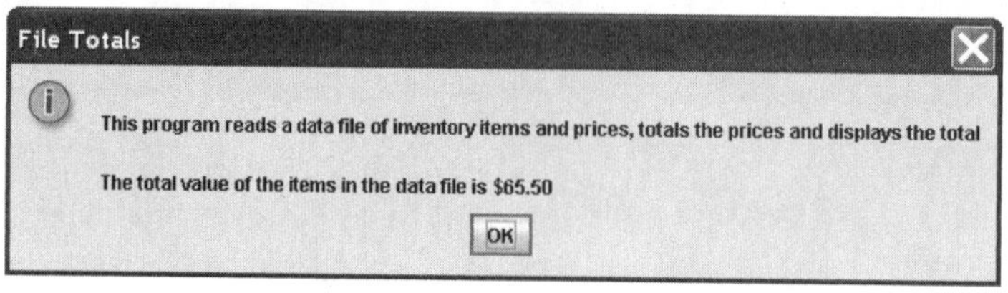

Figure 5-3   File Totals dialog box

Write your design in the following space. Your design should be a list describing what happens at each line in the program, or should use the format your instructor requires.

4. b.   Write a Java program based on the design that you created in Exercise 4a.

   After entering your code but before executing your program, step through your code by hand and complete a memory chart showing what occurs in memory when the Java code is executed.

   To fill out the memory chart for each variable, specify the name of the variable, its data type, the line number in which the variable is assigned its initial value, the initial value assigned to the variable, and the line numbers in which the variable's value changes. If all of the line numbers in which the variable's value changes will not fit on one memory chart line, use as many lines as needed to specify the line numbers.

Variable name	Data type	Declaration line number	Initialization line number	Initial value	Change line number

   Save the program as **Order1.java** to the device or location specified by your instructor, and then compile, run, and test the program. Test your program with the file **invoice1.dat**. Either copy the dialog boxes that appear and paste them into a document or print screens of the dialog boxes.

   Print your output file and program and attach them to your printed output screens to submit with your work.

LAB 5.2 USING THE for LOOPING (REPETITION) STRUCTURE

The for looping structure, sometimes called a *counted* or *indexed for loop*, is a specialized form of the while loop that you can use to simplify writing counter-controlled loops.

To use the for looping structure, you write a for statement, where the reserved word for is followed by the *initial expression*, *logical expression*, and *update expression* enclosed within parentheses. The program executes a for loop in the following sequence:

1. The initial expression executes.

2. The logical expression is evaluated. If the logical expression is false, the for loop has completed; go to the statement that immediately follows the end of the for loop. (This means that the body of the loop might never be executed.)

3. The body of the loop executes.

4. The update expression executes.

5. Go back to Step 2.

Objectives

In this lab, you create programs that use the for loop.

After completing this lab, you will be able to:

- Write a for loop with an increment update expression.

- Write a for loop with a decrement update expression.

Estimated completion time: **50–60 minutes**

Using the for Looping (Repetition) Structure

Design and write programs using for loops.

1. a. Design a program that uses a for loop to calculate the factorial value entered by a user. The *factorial* of a given positive integer, *n*, is the product of every integer from 1 to *n*, inclusive. For instance, 3 factorial is 3 * 2 * 1, or the value 6. The user should be prompted to enter the number for which the factorial is to be calculated. Calculate the factorial value and display the result of the calculation. If a nonpositive number is entered, display a message that the user must enter a positive number.

   Hint: It is not necessary to multiply by 1. So, you can initialize your loop counter to 2. Test your loop counter to be less than or equal to the number entered. Increment your loop counter. Initialize your answer to 1. Multiply your answer by your counter in each iteration of the loop.

   Following is a copy of the screen results that might appear after running your program, depending on the data entered. The input entered by the user is shown in bold.

   ```
   This program asks the user for a positive integer number,
   computes the factorial value, and displays the answer.
   Please enter a positive number: 5
   The factorial of 5 is 120
   ```

   Write your design in the following space. Your design should be a list of Java comments without any code.

1. b.   Write a Java program based on the design that you created in Exercise 1a. After entering your code but before executing your program, step through your code by hand and complete a memory chart showing what occurs in memory when the Java code is executed.

To fill out the memory chart for each variable, specify the name of the variable, its data type, the line number in which the variable is assigned its initial value, the initial value assigned to the variable, and the line numbers in which the variable's value changes. If all of the line numbers in which the variable's value changes will not fit on one memory chart line, use as many lines as needed to specify the line numbers.

Variable name	Data type	Declaration line number	Initialization line number	Initial value	Change line number

Save the program as **CalcFac1.java** to the device or location specified by your instructor, and then compile, run, and test the program. Test your program with the following input:

5

Copy the instructions, input, and output that are displayed, and paste them in a block comment at the end of your program. Then print your program to submit with your work.

2. a.   Redesign Exercise 1 to calculate a factorial number using a `for` loop, which initializes the loop counter to the factorial value input by the user, and then decrements the counter.

Following is a copy of the screen results that might appear after running your program, depending on the data entered. The input entered by the user is shown in bold.

```
This program asks the user for a positive integer number,
computes the factorial value, and displays the answer.
Please enter a positive number: 5
The factorial of 5 is 120
```

Write your design in the following space. Your design should be a list of Java comments without any code.

2. b. Write a Java program based on the design that you created in Exercise 2a. After entering your code but before executing your program, step through your code by hand and complete a memory chart showing what occurs in memory when the Java code is executed.

To fill out the memory chart for each variable, specify the name of the variable, its data type, the line number in which the variable is assigned its initial value, the initial value assigned to the variable, and the line numbers in which the variable's value changes. If all of the line numbers in which the variable's value changes will not fit on one memory chart line, use as many lines as needed to specify the line numbers.

Variable name	Data type	Declaration line number	Initialization line number	Initial value	Change line number

Save the program as **CalcFac2.java** to the device or location specified by your instructor, and then compile, run, and test the program. Test your program with the following input:

5

Copy the instructions, input, and output that are displayed, and then paste them in a block comment at the end of your program. Then print your program to submit with your work.

LAB 5.3 USING THE do...while LOOPING REPETITION STRUCTURE

The third repetition structure is the do...while loop. The do...while loop differs from both the while loop and the for loop. The while loop and the for loop are called *pretest loops* because the loop condition is evaluated before the loop begins. In both the while loop and the for loop, the body of the loop might be skipped (that is, might not be executed at all) depending on the result of the condition.

The do...while loop is a *posttest loop*. This means that the loop condition is tested at the end of the loop body; therefore, the body of a do...while loop will always be executed at least once.

Objectives

In this lab, you create programs that use the do...while loop.

After completing this lab, you will be able to:

- Write a do...while counter-controlled loop when you know exactly how many pieces of data need to be read.

- Write a do...while sentinel-controlled loop that uses a special sentinel value to end the loop.

- Write a do...while flag-controlled loop that uses a Boolean variable as a decision maker, and evaluates to false to end the loop.

- Write a do...while EOF-controlled loop that continues until the program reaches the end of the file.

Estimated completion time: **20–30 minutes**

Using the do...while Looping Repetition Structure

Rewrite code for the programs you designed in Lab 5.1 using a do...while loop instead of a while loop.

1. a. Redesign the program you created in Lab 5.1 Exercise 1 using a do...while loop. The user should be prompted to enter the number of students enrolled in a course. If the number of students is greater than 0, use a counter-controlled do...while loop to prompt the user to enter the names of the students registered for the class. Create an output file that contains the names of the students in the class. Display a message to the user when the program is complete.

Validate the input value to make sure it is greater than 0.

Following is a copy of the screen results that might appear after running your program, depending on the data entered. The input entered by the user is in bold.

```
This program asks the user to enter the
number and names of students in a course.

How many students are registered for this class? 10

Enter the student's name: George Smith
Enter the student's name: Elaine Sanders
Enter the student's name: Jack Cunningham
Enter the student's name: Susie Brown
Enter the student's name: Marvella Garcia
Enter the student's name: Tony Peterson
```

```
Enter the student's name: John Jones
Enter the student's name: Mary Evans
Enter the student's name: Nancy Drew
Enter the student's name: Lola Zapata

The class is full.
```

Write your design in the following space. Your design should be a list of Java comments without any code.

1. b.   Write a Java program based on the design you created in Exercise 1a. Enter your program and name it **Roster2.java**. Name your output file **student2.dat**.

Step through your code by hand and complete a memory chart showing what occurs in memory when the Java code is executed.

To fill out the memory chart for each variable, specify the name of the variable, its data type, the line number in which the variable is assigned its initial value, the initial value assigned to the variable, and the line numbers in which the variable's value changes. If all of the line numbers in which the variable's value changes will not fit on one memory chart line, use as many lines as needed to specify the line numbers.

Variable name	Data type	Declaration line number	Initialization line number	Initial value	Change line number

Execute your program. Then copy the output and save it in a block comment at the end of your program. Save your source code and output data file to the device or location specified by your instructor.

The output file should list student names. Print your output file and attach it to your work.

2. a.   Redesign the program you created in Lab 5.1 Exercise 2 that creates an invoice using a `do...while` loop. When an order is completed, a bar with a UPC code of 999 is placed on the conveyor belt and also is scanned. When the bar is scanned, an invoice is created that contains all items scanned (except the bar). The invoice is written to an output file for further processing later. Recall that the UPC code of 999 is used as the sentinel value. The output file contains the product name on one line followed by the price of each item on the next line. Prompt the user to scan the next item. Display a message and then the number of items that have been scanned when the value 999 is read.

Following is a copy of the screen results that might appear after running your program, depending on the data entered. The input entered by the user is shown in bold.

```
This order-processing program simulates using a
code reader to scan an item and create an invoice.

Please scan the name of the first item: hammer
Please scan the price of the hammer: 9.95
Please scan the name of the next item: saw
Please scan the price of the saw: 20.15
Please scan the name of the next item: shovel
Please scan the price of the shovel: 35.40
Please scan the name of the next item: 999

3 items scanned.
```

Write your design in the following space. Your design should be a list of Java comments without any code.

2. b.   Write a Java program based on the design you created in Exercise 1a. Enter your program and name it **Scan2.java**. Name your output file **invoice2.dat**.

Step through your code by hand and complete a memory chart showing what occurs in memory when the Java code is executed.

To fill out the memory chart for each variable, specify the name of the variable, its data type, the line number in which the variable is assigned its initial value, the initial value assigned to the variable, and the line numbers in which the variable's value changes. If all of the line numbers in which the variable's value changes will not fit on one memory chart line, use as many lines as needed to specify the line numbers.

Variable name	Data type	Declaration line number	Initialization line number	Initial value	Change line number

Execute your program. Test your program with the following input:

```
hammer
9.95
saw
20.15
shovel
35.40
999
```

Copy the output and save it in a block comment at the end of your program. Save your source code and output data file to the device or location specified by your instructor. Print your output file and attach it to your work.

3. a.   *Critical Thinking Exercise*: Redesign the program you created in Lab 5.1 Exercise 3 to create an invoice using a flag-controlled do...while loop with a compound conditional expression that utilizes the Boolean variable found and the Scanner method hasNext(). The file **invoice2.dat** created in Exercise 2 lists descriptions of items on one line followed by the price of the item on the next line. The program should prompt the user to enter an item. The item entered will be used to search a list in the **invoice2.dat** file until the program finds the item in the list or the end-of-file is reached. If the item is found, display the name and price of the item. If the item is not found, display the message that the item was not in the list. Format the price to show two decimal places.

Figure 5-4 shows the screen results that might appear after running your program, depending on the data entered.

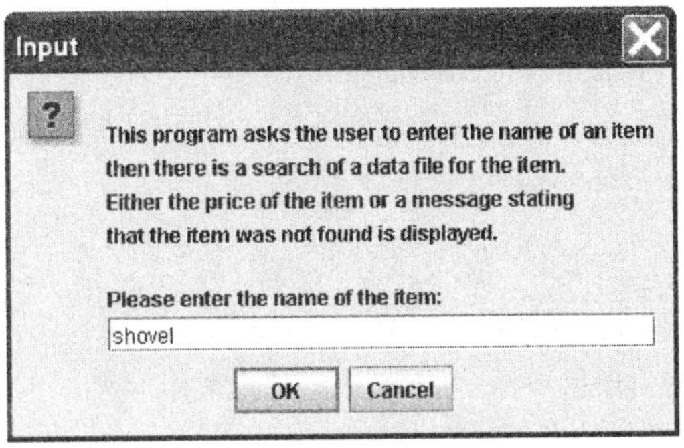

Figure 5-4   Input dialog box for search program

Depending on the string entered and the data in the file, the output would resemble Figure 5-5.

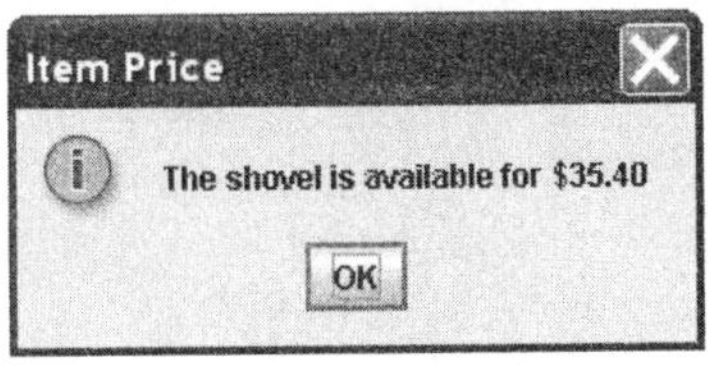

Figure 5-5   Item Price dialog box for search program

Write your design in the following space. Your design should be a list of Java comments without any code.

3. b. Write a Java program based on the design that you created in Exercise 3a. After entering your code but before executing your program, step through your code by hand and complete a memory chart showing what occurs in memory when the Java code is executed.

To fill out the memory chart for each variable, specify the name of the variable, its data type, the line number in which the variable is assigned its initial value, the initial value assigned to the variable, and the line numbers in which the variable's value changes. If all of the line numbers in which the variable's value changes will not fit on one memory chart line, use as many lines as needed to specify the line numbers.

Variable name	Data type	Declaration line number	Initialization line number	Initial value	Change line number

Save the program as **Find2.java** to the device or location specified by your instructor, and then compile, run, and test the program. Either copy the dialog boxes that appear and paste them into a document or print screens of the dialog boxes.

Test your program with the file **invoice2.dat** and with the following input:

```
shovel
```

Print your output file and program and attach them to your printed output screens to submit with your work.

4. a.   Redesign the program you created in Lab 5.1 Exercise 4 that considers the data file you created and processed in Exercises 2 and 3. Use a `do...while` loop instead of a `while` loop. Read all of the data from the file **invoice2.dat** and calculate the total price of all of the items. Because all data is read from a file, there are no prompts or input from the user. Display your data in currency format.

Depending on the information in the file, the output should resemble Figure 5-6.

Figure 5-6   File Totals dialog box for second program

Write your design in the following space. Your design should be a list of Java comments without any code.

4. b. Write a Java program based on the design that you created in Exercise 4a.

After entering your code but before executing your program, step through your code by hand and complete a memory chart showing what occurs in memory when the Java code is executed.

To fill out the memory chart for each variable, specify the name of the variable, its data type, the line number in which the variable is assigned its initial value, the initial value assigned to the variable, and the line numbers in which the variable's value changes. If all of the line numbers in which the variable's value changes will not fit on one memory chart line, use as many lines as needed to specify the line numbers.

Variable name	Data type	Declaration line number	Initialization line number	Initial value	Change line number

Save the program as **Order2.java** to the device or location specified by your instructor, and then compile, run, and test the program. Test your program with the file **invoice2.dat**. Either copy the dialog boxes that appear and paste them into a document or print screens of the dialog boxes.

Print your output file and program and attach them to your printed output screens to submit with your work.

LAB 5.4 USING break AND continue STATEMENTS

The break and continue statements alter the flow of control in a program. When you use a break in a switch statement or in a repetition structure, you provide an immediate exit from the structure. The program continues to execute with the first statement after the structure.

Use a continue statement in a repetition structure to end the current iteration only and proceed with the next iteration of the loop. In a for loop, the next statement is the update statement. Use a break statement in a repetition structure to end the entire repetition. Use these constructs sparingly. They are introduced for informational purposes, but are not suggested for general solutions.

Objectives

In this lab, you use break and continue statements to alter the control of a loop.

After completing this lab, you will be able to:

- Execute a loop until a break statement is encountered.

- Execute a loop and skip over the remaining loop statement when a continue statement is encountered and proceed in the loop until the loop terminates.

Estimated completion time: **20–30 minutes**

Using break and continue Statements

In the following exercises, you evaluate the output in repetition control structures that use the continue or break statements. You also write programs from designs that use the continue or break statements.

1. a. Design a program that uses a for loop to enter 20 numbers and add those that are positive. Use the continue statement if the number entered is not positive. This will result in only the positive numbers being summed and the negative numbers being ignored. The user is to be prompted to enter the numbers. Display the total.

Following is a copy of the screen results that might appear after running your program, depending on the data entered. The input entered by the user is shown in bold.

```
This program asks the user to enter 20 numbers,
adds the positive numbers, and displays the totals.
Please enter 20 numbers; separate each with a space:
2 3 1 -6 10 2 6 5 9 -10 9 2 -4 3 1 2 -6 7 3 2
The sum of the positive numbers is: 67
```

Write your design in the following space. Your design should be a list of Java comments without any code.

1. b. Write a Java program based on the design you created in Exercise 1a. Enter your program and name it **Sum.java**. Step through your code by hand and complete a memory chart showing what occurs in memory when the Java code is executed.

   To fill out the memory chart for each variable, specify the name of the variable, its data type, the line number in which the variable is assigned its initial value, the initial value assigned to the variable, and the line numbers in which the variable's value changes. If all of the line numbers in which the variable's value changes will not fit on one memory chart line, use as many lines as needed to specify the line numbers.

Variable name	Data type	Declaration line number	Initialization line number	Initial value	Change line number

   Execute your program. Test your program with the following input:

   ```
   2 3 1 -6 10 2 6 5 9 -10 9 2 -4 3 1 2 -6 7 3 2
   ```

   Copy the instructions, input, and output that are displayed, and then paste them in a block comment at the end of your program. Save your source code and output data file to the device or location specified by your instructor. Print your program to submit with your work.

2. a. Redesign the program that you created in Lab 5.4 Exercise 1 using a **break** statement instead of the **continue** statement. This will result in only the positive values being summed until the first negative value is encountered. Then the program should not consider any more values.

   Following is a copy of the screen results that might appear after running your program, depending on the data entered. The input entered by the user is shown in bold.

   ```
   This program asks the user to enter 20 numbers,
   adds the positive numbers until the first negative
   value is encountered, and displays the totals.
   Please enter 20 numbers; separate each with a space:
   2 3 1 -6 10 2 6 5 9 -10 9 2 -4 3 1 2 -6 7 3 2
   The sum of the numbers entered until a negative number is entered is: 6
   ```

   Write your design in the following space. Your design should be a list of Java comments without any code.

2. b. Write a Java program based on the design you created in Exercise 2a. Enter your program and name it **SumwBrk.java**. Step through your code by hand and complete a memory chart showing what occurs in memory when the Java code is executed.

To fill out the memory chart for each variable, specify the name of the variable, its data type, the line number in which the variable is assigned its initial value, the initial value assigned to the variable, and the line numbers in which the variable's value changes. If all of the line numbers in which the variable's value changes will not fit on one memory chart line, use as many lines as needed to specify the line numbers.

Variable name	Data type	Declaration line number	Initialization line number	Initial value	Change line number

Execute your program. Test your program with the following input:

```
2 3 1 -6 10 2 6 5 9 -10 9 2 -4 3 1 2 -6 7 3 2
```

Copy the instructions, input, and output that are displayed, and then paste them in a block comment at the end of your program. Save your source code and output data file to the device or location specified by your instructor. Print your program to submit with your work.

LAB 5.5 USING NESTED CONTROL STRUCTURES

One control structure can be nested (contained) within another control structure, that structure can be nested within another control structure, and so on. The control structures do not have to be of the same type.

Inner control structures close before the outer control structure (that is, the containing control structure) closes.

Objectives

In this lab, you use a nested control structure within a control structure.

After completing this lab, you will be able to:

- Recognize the beginning and end of control structures.

- When an inner control structure is a `for` loop, recognize that the loop is reinitialized with each iteration of an outer loop.

Estimated completion time: **40–50 minutes**

Using Nested Control Structures

In the following exercises, you design and write programs that use nested control structures.

1. a. Design a Java program that asks a user to enter a character and a sentence. The program counts the number of times the character entered appears in the sentence. Display a message that tells how often the specified character appears in the sentence.

   Figures 5-7 and 5-8 show the screen results that might appear after running your program, depending on the data entered.

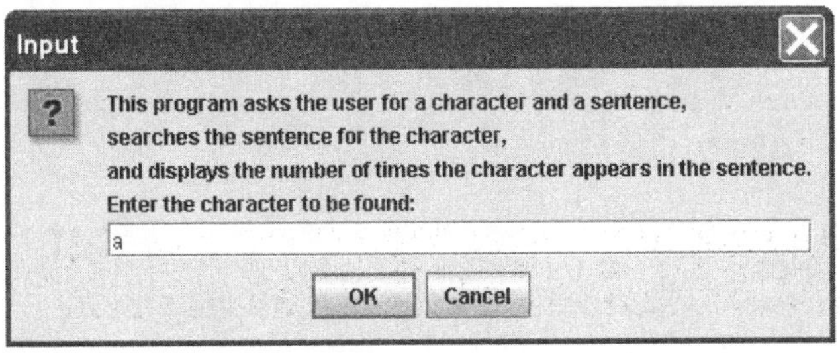

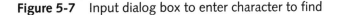

Figure 5-7   Input dialog box to enter character to find

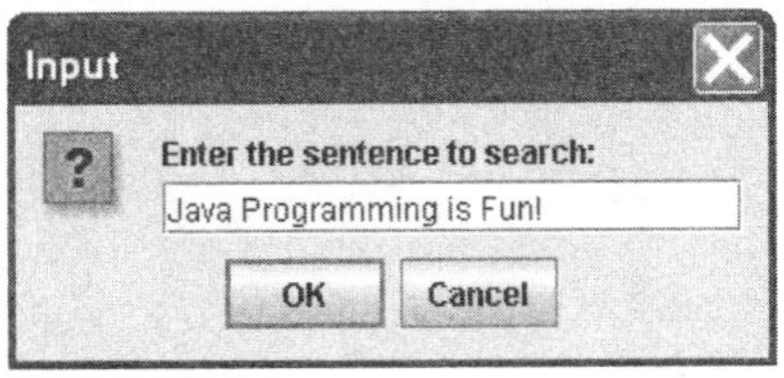

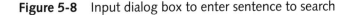

Figure 5-8   Input dialog box to enter sentence to search

Depending on the string entered, the output would resemble Figure 5-9.

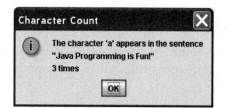

Figure 5-9   Character Count dialog box

Write your design in the following space. Your design should be a list of Java comments without any code.

1. b. Write a Java program based on the design you created in Exercise 1a. Enter your program and name it **ChCount1.java**. Step through your code by hand and complete a memory chart showing what occurs in memory when the Java code is executed.

To fill out the memory chart for each variable, specify the name of the variable, its data type, the line number in which the variable is assigned its initial value, the initial value assigned to the variable, and the line numbers in which the variable's value changes. If all of the line numbers in which the variable's value changes will not fit on one memory chart line, use as many lines as needed to specify the line numbers.

Variable name	Data type	Declaration line number	Initialization line number	Initial value	Change line number

Save **ChCount1.java** to the device or location specified by your instructor, and then compile, run, and test the program. Either copy the dialog boxes that appear and paste them into a document or print screens of the dialog boxes.

Test your program with the following input:

Character to enter: `'a'`

Sentence to enter: `"Java Programming is Fun!"`

Print your output file and program and attach them to your printed output screens to submit with your work.

2. a. *Critical Thinking Exercise*: Redesign the program that you created in Lab 5.5 Exercise 1 to allow the user to enter additional sentences. Create an outer loop that asks the user if he or she would like to enter another sentence. The outer loop should continue as long as the user answers 'y'. Remember to reinitialize your character counter each time you go through your outer loop. You will need one more prompt to ask users if they want to enter another sentence.

Figures 5-10 and 5-11 show the screen results that might appear after running your program, depending on the data entered.

Figure 5-10   Entering the character to find

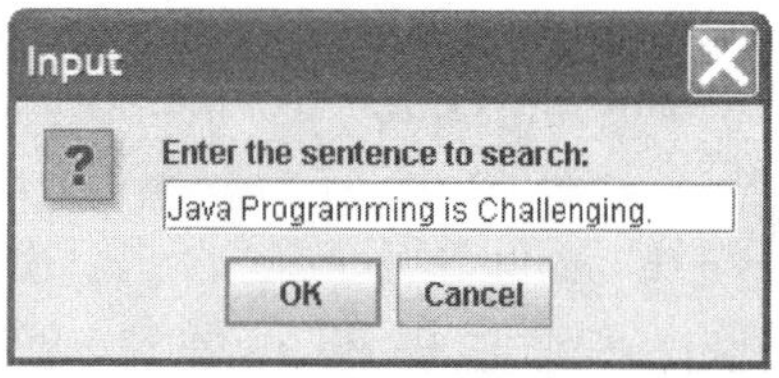

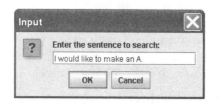

Figure 5-11 Entering the sentence to search

Depending on the string entered and the data in the file, the output would resemble Figures 5–12 through 5–16.

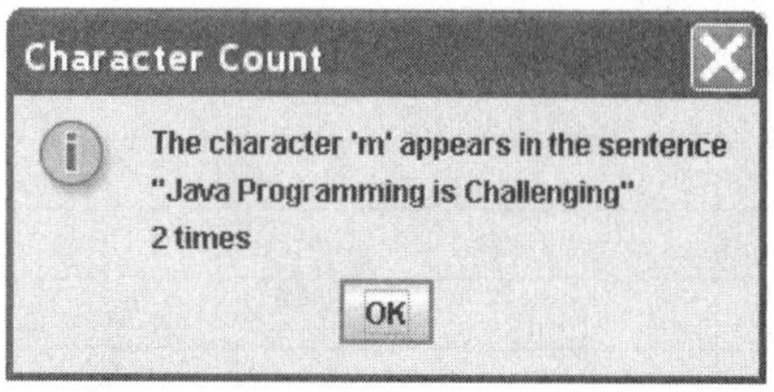

Figure 5-12 Character Count dialog box for second program

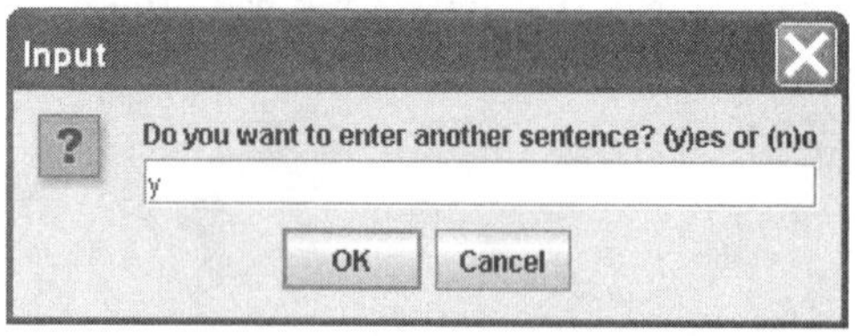

Figure 5-13 First Input dialog box

Figure 5-14 Second Input dialog box

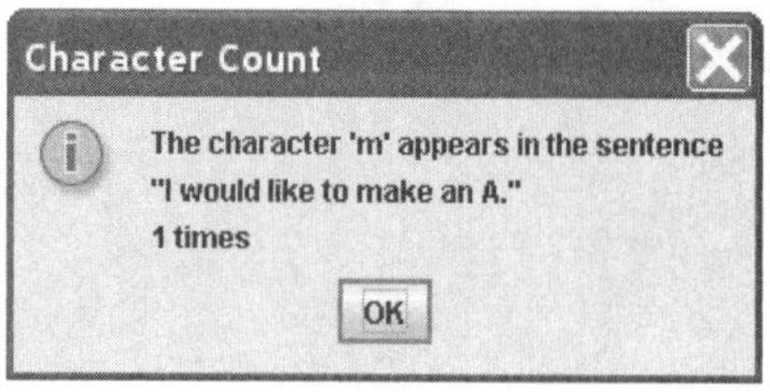

Figure 5-15 Results of second test

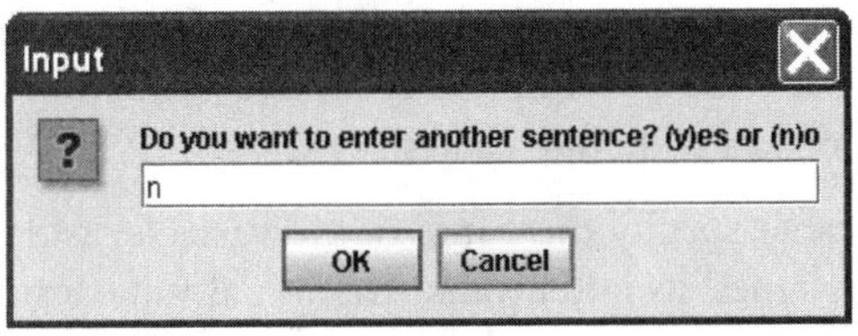

Figure 5-16   Third Input dialog box

Write your design in the following space. Your design should be a list of Java comments without any code.

2. b. Write a Java program based on the design you created in Exercise 2a. Enter your program and name it **ChCount2.java**. Step through your code by hand and complete a memory chart showing what occurs in memory when the Java code is executed.

To fill out the memory chart for each variable, specify the name of the variable, its data type, the line number in which the variable is assigned its initial value, the initial value assigned to the variable, and the line numbers in which the variable's value changes. If all of the line numbers in which the variable's value changes will not fit on one memory chart line, use as many lines as needed to specify the line numbers.

Variable name	Data type	Declaration line number	Initialization line number	Initial value	Change line number

Save **ChCount2.java** to the device or location specified by your instructor, and then compile, run, and test the program. Either copy the dialog boxes that appear and paste them into a document or print screens of the dialog boxes.

Test your program with the following input:

Character to enter: `'m'`

Sentence to enter: `"Java Programming is Challenging."`

Answer to enter: `y`

Sentence to enter: `"I would like to make an A."`

Answer to enter: `n`

Print your output file and program and attach them to your printed output screens to submit with your work.

3. a. *Critical Thinking Exercise*: Design a program that prints column titles and row titles in a spreadsheet format. The values 1, 2, 3, 4, 5 should appear in the first five columns of the first five rows. Use a **for** loop to output the column headings. Use nested **for** loops to output the row number and the values within the rows and columns. The output should look like the following.

```
     A     B     C     D     E
1    1     2     3     4     5
2    1     2     3     4     5
3    1     2     3     4     5
4    1     2     3     4     5
5    1     2     3     4     5
```

Write your design in the following space. Your design should be a list of Java comments without any code.

3. b. Write a Java program based on the design you created in Exercise 3a. Enter your program and name it **Table.java**. Step through your code by hand and complete a memory chart showing what occurs in memory when the Java code is executed.

To fill out the memory chart for each variable, specify the name of the variable, its data type, the line number in which the variable is assigned its initial value, the initial value assigned to the variable, and the line numbers in which the variable's value changes. If all of the line numbers in which the variable's value changes will not fit on one memory chart line, use as many lines as needed to specify the line numbers.

Variable name	Data type	Declaration line number	Initialization line number	Initial value	Change line number

Execute your program. Then copy the output and save it in a block comment at the end of your program. Save your source code and output data file to the device or location specified by your instructor.

CHAPTER

6

GRAPHICAL USER INTERFACE (GUI) AND OBJECT-ORIENTED DESIGN (OOD)

In this chapter, you will:

♦ Learn about basic GUI components

♦ Explore how the GUI components `JFrame`, `JLabel`, `JTextField`, and `JButton` work

♦ Become familiar with the concept of event-driven programming

♦ Discover events and event handlers

♦ Explore object-oriented design

♦ Learn how to identify objects, classes, and members of a class

♦ Learn about wrapper classes

♦ Become familiar with autoboxing and unboxing of primitive data types

123

CHAPTER 6: ASSIGNMENT COVER SHEET

Name _____   Date _____

Section _____

Lab Assignments	Grade
Lab 6.1 Extending the GUI Component JFrame	
Lab 6.2 Accessing the Content Pane	
Lab 6.3 Using an Event Handler (Critical Thinking Exercises)	
Lab 6.4 Using Object-Oriented Design	
Lab 6.5 Implementing Classes and Operations (Critical Thinking Exercises)	
Total Grade	

See your instructor or the introduction to this book for instructions on submitting your assignments.

Write your design in the following space. Your design should be a list of Java comments without any code.

1. b.   Write a Java program based on the design you created in Exercise 1a. Enter your program and name it **PropertyTax3.java**. Save the program to the device or location specified by your instructor.

Lab 6.4 Using Object-Oriented Design

Object-oriented design (OOD) uses objects to design programs. To use an object, you do not need to know the makeup of the object. This information might be hidden from you. However, you need to know the functions of the object (such as buttons) and how to use them. You can use an object by itself or with other objects, but you cannot modify the functions of the object. To create objects, you first need to learn to create classes; to know what type of classes to create, you need to know what an object stores and what operations are needed to manipulate an object's data.

The aim of OOD is to build software from software components called classes and to use the various methods provided by those classes. In OOD, you first identify the object, then identify the relevant data, and then identify operations needed to manipulate that data. One basic principle of OOD is *encapsulation*—the ability to combine data, and operations on that data, in a single unit.

OOD methodology can be expressed in the following steps:

1. Write a detailed description of the problem.

2. Identify all (relevant) nouns and verbs.

3. From the list of nouns, select objects. Identify data components of each object.

4. From the list of verbs, select the operations on objects and their data.

Objectives

In this lab, you read a problem and identify the components of the problem using the OOD methodology steps.

After completing this lab, you will be able to:

- Separate a problem statement into OOD methodology steps.
- Identify all nouns.
- Identify classes.
- Identify data members for each of the classes.
- Identify operations for each of the classes.

Estimated completion time: **20–30 minutes**

Using Object-Oriented Design

Consider the following problem:

Company XYZ needs a program to build a database concerning employee information. The program should do the following:

- Ask employees for their name and number of dependents claimed for tax purposes.
- Display a message to verify the number of tax deductions. (This will be one more than the number of dependents entered.)
- Let employees select whether they want personal health insurance or family health insurance.
- Display a message to verify the selection and tell each employee the cost of the selection.
- Let employees select whether they want to deduct union dues from their paycheck.
- Display a message to verify the selection and tell each employee the cost of the selection.
- Show the OOD solution of this problem.

Step 1: Identify all nouns.

Step 2: Identify clas s).

Step 3: Identify data members for each of the classes.

Step 4: Identify operations for each of the objects (classes).

LAB 6.5 IMPLEMENTING CLASSES AND OPERATIONS

After you define relevant classes, data members, and relevant operations, the next step is to implement these in Java. To implement operations in Java, you write algorithms. Each algorithm is implemented with the help of Java's methods. Sometimes, the data you are given belongs to the primitive data types, but objects are needed by the methods. Java provides the classes `Integer`, `Double`, `Character`, `Long`, and `Float` so that values of primitive data types can be treated as objects. These classes are called *wrappers*.

To simplify the use of wrapper class objects, primitive values can be *autoboxed* (automatically converted to wrapper objects), and wrapper objects can be *auto-unboxed* (automatically converted to primitive values).

Included with this text are the classes `IntClass` and `DoubleClass`, which are similar to the classes `Integer` and `Double`, respectively. They are found with your Chapter 7 student files. The constructor methods are used to initialize the objects that are instantiated. The method `setNum( )` is used to set the data member to its parameter value. The method `getNum( )` is used to retrieve a value. The method `addToNum( )` is used to update the data value by its parameter value. The method `compareTo( )` compares the data value with the parameter value. The method `equals( )` compares the data value with the parameter value. The method `toString( )` converts the value to a string.

Objectives

In this lab, you write a program based on the OOD design you developed in Lab 6.4 to create information for an employee database. Display a window with five rows and three columns.

After completing this lab, you will be able to:

- Implement a Java program from an OOD.

- Use the `IntClass` in a Java program.

> Estimated completion time: **50–60 minutes**

Implementing Classes and Operations

In the following exercises, you write a program from an OOD design and use the user-defined `IntClass`.

Critical Thinking Exercise: Write a Java program based on the design you created in Lab 6.4. Enter your program and name it **EmployeeInfo.java**. Following is a copy of the screen results that might appear after running your program.

Figure 6-4   Employee Information window

Save the program to the device or location specified by your instructor, and then compile, run, and test the program. Either copy the dialog box that appears and paste it into a document or print the screen of the dialog box.

Test your program with the following input:

Employee Name: **Hakim Maddulah**

Number of Dependents: **3**

Health Insurance 1 self, 2 family: **2**

Union Dues 0 none, 1 yes: **1**

USER-DEFINED METHODS

In this chapter, you will:

- ◆ Understand how methods are used in Java programming
- ◆ Explore predefined methods and how to use them in a program
- ◆ Learn about user-defined methods
- ◆ Examine value-returning methods
- ◆ Understand actual and formal parameters
- ◆ Explore how to construct and use a value-returning, user-defined method in a program
- ◆ Learn how to construct and use user-defined void methods in a program
- ◆ Explore variables as parameters
- ◆ Learn about the scope of an identifier
- ◆ Become acquainted with method overloading

CHAPTER 7: ASSIGNMENT COVER SHEET

Name _____   Date _____

Section _____

Lab Assignments	Grade
Lab 7.1 Using Predefined Methods in a Program	
Lab 7.2 Designing and Implementing a Program Using Predefined, Value-Returning Methods	
Lab 7.3 Implementing Value-Returning, User-Defined Methods in a Program	
Lab 7.4 Designing and Implementing Value-Returning, User-Defined Methods in a Program (Critical Thinking Exercises)	
Lab 7.5 Designing and Implementing void User-Defined Methods with No Parameters, Primitive Type Parameters, and String Parameters (Critical Thinking Exercises)	
Lab 7.6 Designing and Implementing void User-Defined Methods with Reference Parameters	
Lab 7.7 Identifying the Scope of an Identifier	
Lab 7.8 Using Method Overloading	
Total Grade	

See your instructor or the introduction to this book for instructions on submitting your assignments.

LAB 7.1 USING PREDEFINED METHODS IN A PROGRAM

A Java program is a collection of classes, and each class is a collection of methods and data members. Some of these classes are predefined, and their methods are designed to perform specific, commonly encountered tasks. For example, `sqrt()` is a method in the predefined class `Math` and is used to calculate square roots. These predefined classes are organized into collections of classes known as *class libraries* or *packages*.

Two commonly used classes are `Math`, which contains predefined methods for performing mathematical operations, and `Character`, which contains predefined methods for character manipulation. To use the predefined methods of these and other classes, you must import the packages that contain the classes.

Objectives

In this lab, you include the correct class library for predefined methods, write method calls to predefined methods, provide the missing code, and test the code. To complete this lab, you need to use the `toLowerCase`, `ceil`, `floor`, and `abs` predefined methods.

After completing this lab, you will be able to:

- Use predefined methods with parameters.

- Write method calls to predefined methods.

- Use values from value-returning, predefined methods.

Estimated completion time: **30–40 minutes**

Using Predefined Methods in a Program

In the following exercise, you complete a Java program that uses the class `Math`.

1. Complete a program that asks the user to enter a floating-point number (either positive or negative). The program repeats while the user enters 'y' to continue. The program allows the user to enter either a lowercase or uppercase character. Use the `ceil()`, `floor()`, and `abs()` methods to determine the smallest whole number that is greater than or equal to the number entered, the largest whole number that is less than or equal to the number entered, and the absolute value of the number given, respectively. Use the `toLowerCase()` method to change a given character value to lowercase if the value is an uppercase value.

   Supply the missing code and import the correct packages for the predefined methods used.

   Following is a copy of the screen results that might appear after running your program, depending on the data entered after all the changes have been made. The text entered by the user appears in bold.

```
Enter a float number and I will tell you:
the smallest whole number >= to the number,
the largest whole number <= to the number,
and the absolute value of the number.

5.4

The smallest whole number greater than 5.4 is 6.0
The largest whole number less than 5.4 is 5.0
The absolute value of 5.4 is 5.4

Do you want to enter more data? y/n
y
```

```
Enter a float number and I will tell you:
the smallest whole number >= to the number,
the largest whole number <= to the number,
and the absolute value of the number.

-8.8

The smallest whole number greater than -8.8 is -8.0
The largest whole number less than -8.8 is -9.0
The absolute value of -8.8 is 8.8


Do you want to enter more data? y/n
n
```

Complete the following Java program, inserting comments, package names, or calls to methods of the class Math after the bold comments. For readability, leave the blank lines and comments in place throughout the program. Save the program as **NumbersFixed.java** to the device or location specified by your instructor. Compile, execute, and test the program. After executing your program, select and copy everything that appears on your screen. Paste the copied text into a comment block at the end of your program.

```java
// Include comments to identify the writer of the code
// and to describe the program.

import java.util.*;
// The following statement imports the Math class.
import

public class NumbersFixed
{
  static Scanner console = new Scanner(System.in);

  public static void main(String[] args)
  {
    double x;
    String token;
    char again = 'y';

    while (again == 'y')
    {
      System.out.println("Enter a float number and I will "
        + "tell you:\n"
        + "the smallest whole number >= to the number,\n"
        + "the largest whole number <= to the number,\n"
        + "and the absolute value of the number.\n");

      x = console.nextDouble();

      System.out.println("\nThe smallest whole number "
        + "greater than " + x + " is "
        // Following is a method call to calculate the
        // smallest whole number >= the input value.
        +
        + "\nThe largest whole number less than " + x
        + " is "
        // Following is a method call to calculate the
        // largest whole number <= the input value.
        +
        + "\nThe absolute value of " + x + " is "
```

```
            // Following is a method call to calculate the
            // absolute value of the input value.
            +
            + "\n");

        System.out.println("Do you want to enter more data?"
            + " y/n ");
        token = console.next();
        again = token.charAt(0);
        // The following statement converts the response
        // character entered by the user to lowercase.
        again =
      }
   }
}
```

LAB 7.2 DESIGNING AND IMPLEMENTING A PROGRAM USING PREDEFINED, VALUE-RETURNING METHODS

Some methods return a value, and those methods are described as being of the data type they return. For example, the pow method of the Math class returns a double value, so we say that *pow is a method of type double*. When using a predefined, value-returning method in a program design, you should specify that method along with a description of its formal parameters and its return type.

Objectives

In this lab, you design and implement a Java program that uses predefined, value-returning methods.

After completing this lab, you will be able to:

- Design and implement a program that uses predefined, value-returning methods with parameters.

- Describe the use of each program module.

Estimated completion time: **50–60 minutes**

Designing and Implementing a Program Using Predefined, Value-Returning Methods

In the following exercises, you answer questions to determine the design of a Java program. Each exercise may have several correct answers. The answers you choose will determine your program design.

1. Suppose a user wants to calculate the square of a number or the square root of a number, and display the results. To design this problem, what do you need to know about the predefined methods that have this purpose?

2. The user will also enter a character value to designate which process is wanted. Should you make any assumptions about the case of the character entered? Would that require using any other predefined method?

3. What variables do you need for user input and for calculations? What types are these variables?

4. The program should process at least one number, and the user should be allowed to continue processing numbers until a value is entered to quit. What kind of loop works best in this situation?

5. Does the numeric value entered need any type of validation? Is that validation dependent on which math method is to be called?

6. What is the required data type and number of arguments required for the predefined methods you are using?

7. If the methods you are using are value returning, how will those returned values be handled?

8. Should your decimal numbers be formatted? If so, what method, from what class, is needed?

9. a. Design the program to calculate either the square of a number or the square root of a number and display the results.

   Following is a copy of the screen results that might appear after running your program, depending on the data entered. The text entered by the user appears in bold.

   ```
   Enter a float value: 6.2
   Do you want the (s)quare or square (r)oot of 6.2: r
   The square root of 6.2 is 2.4899799195977463

   Do you want to enter more data? y/n: y
   Enter a float value: -4.6
   Do you want the (s)quare or square (r)oot of -4.6: r
   You must have a positive number for square root.
   Do you want the (s)quare or square (r)oot of -4.6: s
   The number -4.6 squared has the value 21.159999999999997

   Do you want to enter more data? y/n: y
   Enter a float value: 3.9
   Do you want the (s)quare or square (r)oot of 3.9: s
   The number 3.9 squared has the value 15.209999999999999

   Do you want to enter more data? y/n: y
   Enter a float value: -4
   Do you want the (s)quare or square (r)oot of -4.0: s
   The number -4.0 squared has the value 16.0

   Do you want to enter more data? y/n: n
   ```

   Write your design in the following space. Your design should be a list of Java comments without any code.

9. b. Write a Java program based on the design you created in Exercise 9a. For readability, insert blank lines to separate parts of the program. Include comments to explain the different sections of code. Save the program as **SqrSqrt.java** to the device or location specified by your instructor. Compile, execute, and test the program. After executing your program, select and copy everything that appears on your screen. Paste the copied text into a comment block at the end of your program.

LAB 7.3 IMPLEMENTING VALUE-RETURNING, USER-DEFINED METHODS IN A PROGRAM

Because Java does not provide every method you might ever need, you can write your own methods, called *user-defined* methods. User-defined methods can be value-returning methods or `void` methods (that is, methods that have a `void` return type and return no value).

Generally, you will call a value-returning method in an expression; the expression can be part of a statement, such as an assignment statement or an output statement. Calling a method causes the statements in the body of the called method to be executed.

The visibility of a method determines where in a program the method can be used (called). The default visibility of a method is *package visibility*. To give a method a different visibility, you specify one of the visibility modifiers `public`, `private`, or `protected`. A *modifier* is an optional Java keyword that modifies how a method or other identifier behaves or can be used. When you write a method, its modifiers appear just before its return data type. Some other modifiers are `static`, `abstract`, and `final`.

This chapter focuses on `public` methods (those that can be called from anywhere in a program) and `private` methods (those that can be called only from other methods of the same class).

A value-returning method returns a value via a `return` statement. The data type of the value returned must either match or be convertible to the return data type specified for the method.

Objectives

In this lab, you complete a program that contains two value-returning, user-defined methods.

After completing this lab, you will be able to:

- Write calls to value-returning, user-defined methods with and without parameters.

- Write value-returning, user-defined methods with and without parameters.

Estimated completion time: **30–40 minutes**

Implementing Value-Returning, User-Defined Methods in a Program

In the following exercises, you examine Java programs that call value-returning, user-defined methods. Value-returning methods can have formal parameters or no parameters.

1. The following program design contains two methods that have a `String` argument that will be used in the methods as a prompt to the user. The method `getValue` returns an integer value and the method `getLetter` returns a character.

   Provide the missing code designated by the comments. Your code should include calls to methods `getValue` and `getLetter` and headings to those methods. The program asks the user for today's year and month, and his or her year and month of birth. The program calculates and displays the user's age and continues when the user enters 'y'.

   Following is a copy of the screen results that might appear after running your program, depending on the data entered. The input entered by the user is in bold.

   ```
   This program asks you to enter today's year in 4 digits.
   Then it asks you to enter today's month number.

   In the next step you will be asked to enter the 4-digit year of your birth.
   ```

```
Then you will be asked to enter the month number of your birth.

The program will calculate and display how old you are in years and months.


Enter today's 4-digit year: 2005
Enter today's month number: 10
Enter the 4-digit year of your birth: 1986
Enter the month number of your birth: 8
You are 19 years and 2 months old.

Do you want to enter more data? y/n n
```

Complete the following Java program, replacing the bold comments with code as appropriate. For readability, insert blank lines to separate parts of the program. Include comments to explain the different sections of code. Save the program as **CalcAge.java** to the device or location specified by your instructor. Compile, execute, and test the program. After executing your program, select and copy everything that appears on your screen. Paste the copied text into a comment block at the end of your program.

```java
// Write comments for programmer identification and to describe
// what the program does.

import java.util.Scanner;
import java.lang.Math;

public class CalcAge
{
  static Scanner console = new Scanner(System.in);

  public static void main(String[] args)
  {
    int currentYear = 0, currentMonth = 0, year, month, age;
    String line;
    char again = 'y';

    System.out.println("This program asks you to enter today's "
      + "year in 4-digits.\n"
      + "Then it asks you to enter today's month number.\n\n"
      + "In the next step you will be asked to enter "
      + "the 4-digit year of your birth.\n"
      + "Then you will be asked to enter the month number "
      + "of your birth.\n\n"
      + "The program will calculate and display how old you "
      + " are in years and months.\n\n");

    while (currentYear < 2002 || currentMonth < 1
      || currentMonth > 12)
    {
      // Call the method getValue with the String argument,
      // "Enter today's 4-digit year: ".
      currentYear =

      if (currentYear < 2002)
        System.out.println("You did not enter current year.\n");
      else
      {
        // Call the method getValue with the String argument,
        // "Enter today's month number: ".
        currentMonth =
```

```
        if (currentMonth < 1 || currentMonth > 12)
          System.out.println("You did not enter a month "
            + "between 1 and 12.\n");
    }
  }

  while (again == 'y')
  {
    // Call the method getValue with the String argument
    // "Enter the 4-digit year of your birth: ".
    year =

    if (year > currentYear || year < 1)
    {
      System.out.println("You did not enter a valid year.\n");
      continue;
    }

    // Call the method getValue with the String argument,
    // "Enter the month number of your birth: ".
    month =

    if (month < 1 || month > 12)
    {
      System.out.println("You did not enter a valid "
        + "month.\n");
      continue;
    }

    if (currentMonth > month)
    {
      age = currentYear - year;
      month = currentMonth - month;
    }

    else if (currentMonth == month)
    {
      age = currentYear - year;
      month = 0;
    }

    else    //currentMonth < month
    {
      age = currentYear - year - 1;
      month = 12 - month + currentMonth;
    }

    if ( (age < 0 || age > 120) || (age == 0 && month < 0) )
    {
      System.out.println("You did not enter valid dates.\n");
      continue;
    }
    System.out.println("You are " + age + " years and "
      + month + " months old.\n");

    // Call the method getLetter with the String argument,
    // "Do you want to enter more data? y/n ".
    again =
  } // end while
}  //end of main
```

```
    // Write the heading for the value-returning method
    // getValue, which has a String formal parameter
    // named message.
    {
      int value;
      System.out.print(message);
      System.out.flush();
      value = console.nextInt();
      return value;
    }  //end of getValue

    // Write the heading for the value-returning method
    // getLetter, which has a String formal parameter
    // named message.
    {
      char letter;
      String line;
      System.out.print(message);
      System.out.flush();
      line = console.next();
      letter = line.charAt(0);
      return letter;
    }  //end of getLetter
} //end of class
```

LAB 7.4 DESIGNING AND IMPLEMENTING VALUE-RETURNING, USER-DEFINED METHODS IN A PROGRAM

Stepwise refinement, also known as *top-down design*, is a technique by which you design the solution to a problem by breaking the problem down into a collection of smaller, simpler problems. If these smaller problems are still too complex, they can be broken down even further. This technique exploits the idea that solving a collection of simple subproblems usually is easier than solving a single, more complex problem.

When you use stepwise refinement to design a program, user-defined methods are a natural way to implement the subproblems of the design. They can also make the debugging process easier to accomplish.

Objectives

In this lab, you design a program using value-returning, user-defined methods.

After completing this lab, you will be able to:

■ Write a design for a program with value-returning, user-defined methods with and without formal parameters.

Estimated completion time: **40–50 minutes**

Designing and Implementing Value-Returning, User-Defined Methods in a Program

In the following exercises, you design and write Java programs that use value-returning, user-defined methods.

1. a. *Critical Thinking Exercise*: Design a program that asks the user to enter a year and then determines if it is a leap year. Be sure to tell the user what the program does. Your program should have a loop and continue when the user enters the character 'y'.

    Write three methods according to the following descriptions:

    ■ `getYear` has no formal parameters, asks the user to enter a year, and returns an integer value that is assigned to the integer variable `year`.

    ■ `isLeap` has an integer formal parameter, year, determines if the year is a leap year, and returns the Boolean value `true` if the year is a leap year and `false` if it is not. A year is a leap year if it is divisible by 4, but is not divisible by 100 except when divisible by 400. (The year 2000 was a leap year.)

    ■ `moreData` has a `String` formal parameter, asks the user to enter a 'y' or 'n' if he or she wants to process another year, and returns a Boolean value that is assigned to the Boolean variable `again`.

    Be sure to include comments and display the results to the user.

    Following is a copy of the screen results that might appear after running your program, depending on the data entered. The input entered by the user is in bold.

    ```
    This program asks you to enter a year in 4 digits.
    The output will indicate whether the year you entered is a leap year.

    Enter a year: 2003
    2003 is not a leap year.
    ```

```
Do you want to enter more data? y/n: y
Enter a year: 2000
2000 is a leap year.

Do you want to enter more data? y/n: y
Enter a year: 1900
1900 is not a leap year.

Do you want to enter more data? y/n: y
Enter a year: 1800
1800 is not a leap year.

Do you want to enter more data? y/n: y
Enter a year: 2004
2004 is a leap year.

Do you want to enter more data? y/n: n
```

Write your design in the following space. Your design should be a list of Java comments without any code.

1. b.   Write a Java program based on the design you created in Exercise 1a. Save the program as
LeapYear.java to the device or location specified by your instructor. Compile, run, and test the
program. Copy the instructions, input, and output that are displayed, and then paste them in a
block comment at the end of your program.

LAB 7.5 DESIGNING AND IMPLEMENTING void USER-DEFINED METHODS WITH NO PARAMETERS, PRIMITIVE TYPE PARAMETERS, AND STRING PARAMETERS

A void *method* is one defined with a return data type of void, so the method does not return a value to its caller. For this reason, void methods are not called as part of an expression; instead, a call to a void method appears as a stand-alone statement. That is, a void method is called for its *effect* rather than its *value*.

Because a void method does not return a value, it does not require a return statement. When execution reaches the end of the method, control automatically returns to the calling method. However, you can use a return statement with no return value specified to immediately return from the method at any point in its execution.

Objectives

In this lab, you write two void methods with no parameters.

After completing this lab, you will be able to:

- Use stepwise refinement as a program design technique.

- Call a void method with no parameters from the main method.

- Write a void method definition that has no parameters.

- Call a void method with parameters from the main method.

- Write a void method definition with parameters.

Estimated completion time: **50–60 minutes**

Designing and Implementing void User-Defined Methods with No Parameters, Primitive Type Parameters, and String Parameters

In the following exercises, you design and write Java programs that use void user-defined methods.

1. a. Design a program that displays instructions for using the program and displays a title for a payroll report. Enhancements made to this program in later exercises will enable it to process a payroll; however, in this exercise, you are designing only a driver method (main), a void method named instructions to tell the user how to use the payroll program, and a void method named reportTitle to display the headings of the report that will be written later. Neither instructions nor reportTitle have parameters.

    Your instructions method should output the following message:

    ```
                    Instructions for Payroll Report Program
    This program calculates a paycheck for each employee.
    A text file containing the following information will be created:
    name, pay rate, hours worked, and tax percentage to be deducted.

    The program will create a report in columnar format showing the
    employee name, hourly rate, number of hours worked, tax rate,
    gross pay, and net pay.

    After all employees are processed, totals will be displayed,
    including total gross amount and total net pay.
    ```

Your `reportTitle` method should output the following:

```
                    Payroll Report

Employee                  Hourly    Hours     Tax      Gross      Net
Name                      Rate      Worked    Rate     Amount     Amount
--------------------      --------  --------  -------- --------   --------
```

Java does not require that you include method definitions in a particular order, but it is standard to put `main` before other method definitions. Be sure to include comments and display the results to the user.

Write your design in the following space. Your design should be a list of Java comments without any code.

1. b.   Write a Java program based on the design you created in Exercise 1a. Save the program as **Payroll1.java** to the device or location specified by your instructor. Compile, run, and test the program. Copy the instructions, input, and output that are displayed, and then paste them in a block comment at the end of your program.

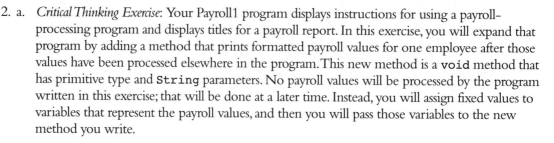

2. a.   *Critical Thinking Exercise*: Your Payroll1 program displays instructions for using a payroll-processing program and displays titles for a payroll report. In this exercise, you will expand that program by adding a method that prints formatted payroll values for one employee after those values have been processed elsewhere in the program. This new method is a `void` method that has primitive type and `String` parameters. No payroll values will be processed by the program written in this exercise; that will be done at a later time. Instead, you will assign fixed values to variables that represent the payroll values, and then you will pass those variables to the new method you write.

In the class definition, declare a floating-point, constant data member named `FULL_TIME` and assign to it the value 40.0. In the `main` method, declare a `String` variable named `employeeName` and `double` variables named `hourlyRate`, `hoursWorked`, `taxRate`, `grossAmount`, and `netAmount`. Because you have not written the payroll-processing code yet, initialize the variables using the following values:

- `employeeName` is assigned the value "Alice Grandell".

- `hourlyRate` is assigned the value 7.75.

- `hoursWorked` is assigned the value 45.0.

- `taxRate` is assigned the value 10.0.

- `grossAmount` is assigned the value 348.75.

- `netAmount` is assigned the value 313.18.

Write a `void` method named `printEmployeeInfo` that has parameters for `employeeName`, `hourlyRate`, `hoursWorked`, `taxRate`, `grossAmount`, and `netAmount`. This method prints the employee's payroll information in columnar format, aligned underneath the appropriate column headings that were printed by the method `reportTitle`. The name should be left-justified in a field that is 20 characters wide. All numeric values should have two digits to the right of the decimal point and be right-justified in a field that is 8 characters wide. If the number of hours worked by the employee is greater than the value of the constant `FULL_TIME`, print the text "OT" (indicating overtime) following the net amount value. Each value should be separated from its neighbors by two spaces. Terminate the output of the method with a newline.

After the call to the `reportTitle` method in the `main` method, write a call to the `printEmployeeInfo` method.

Your `printEmployeeInfo` method should print the following:

```
Alice Grandell        7.75     45.00     10.00     348.75     313.18  OT
```

Your program should print the following:

```
            Instructions for Payroll Report Program
This program calculates a paycheck for each employee.
A text file containing the following information will be created:
name, pay rate, hours worked, and tax percentage to be deducted.

The program will create a report in columnar format showing the
employee name, hourly rate, number of hours worked, tax rate,
gross pay, and net pay.

After all employees are processed, totals will be displayed,
including total gross amount and total net pay.
```

```
                           Payroll Report

Employee          Hourly    Hours      Tax     Gross     Net
Name              Rate      Worked     Rate    Amount    Amount
----------------  --------  --------  --------  --------  --------
Alice Grandell       7.75     45.00     10.00    348.75    313.18  OT
```

Be sure to include comments and display the results to the user.

Write your design in the following space. Your design should be a list of Java comments without any code.

2. b.   Write a Java program based on the design you created in Exercise 2a. Save the program as **Payroll2.java** to the device or location specified by your instructor. Compile, run, and test the program. Copy the instructions, input, and output that are displayed, and paste them in a block comment at the end of your program.

LAB 7.6 DESIGNING AND IMPLEMENTING void USER-DEFINED METHODS WITH REFERENCE PARAMETERS

A formal parameter of a primitive type receives a copy of the value of the corresponding actual parameter (argument) when a method is called. This is known as *call-by-value*. If the method changes the value of the formal parameter, it only changes the copy, not the original (that is, the actual parameter); when control returns from the method, the value of the actual parameter is unchanged, and the copy held in the formal parameter is discarded.

However, a formal parameter that is a reference variable receives the memory location (the memory address) of the object referenced by the actual parameter. That is, the formal parameter and the actual parameter actually refer to (point to) the same object in memory. This is known as *call-by-reference*. So, changing a value within an object referenced by a formal parameter in the method also changes the object referenced by its corresponding actual parameter because they are the same object. This is one way to communicate values from a method back to its caller.

String values are objects, so they are passed to methods using call-by-reference. However, the value of a String object cannot be changed so that a new value can be communicated back to the caller. That is, the value of a String object is *immutable* or unchangeable. If you want to change the value of a string parameter, then you should instead specify the parameter to be of the class StringBuffer, which is a class for manipulating *mutable* string objects. As strange as it might seem, you cannot use an assignment operator on StringBuffer variables, but the class does contain methods for performing append, delete, and other string-manipulation operations.

Objectives

In this lab, you write a void method with reference parameters. Using stepwise refinement, you continue to build on the payroll program. You also create a text file of data to use in payroll processing.

After completing this lab, you will be able to:

- Call a void method with reference parameters from the main method.

- Write a void method definition with reference parameters.

Estimated completion time: **50–60 minutes**

Designing and Implementing void User-Defined Methods with Object Parameters

In the following exercises, you design and write Java programs that use void user-defined methods with reference parameters.

1. Create a text file to contain the data to process. You can use any text editor to create the file, but be sure to save it in a text format. Use the following data and create a text file called **payroll.dat**:

John Smith

9.45 40 15

Jane Doe

12.50 45 15

Harry Morgan

20.00 40 20

Carmen Martinez

25.00 35 25

Jacintha Washington

50.85 60 34

2. a.   Further enhance the program design for your payroll program. Add into the design a Boolean method named `inputData` that has reference parameters to input an employee name, hourly rate, hours worked, and tax rate from the **payroll.dat** file. After the statement within the method `main` that calls the method `reportTitle`, add a loop that allows the program to read, process, and print information for multiple employees until all data has been read and processed. The program you write in this exercise does not calculate the `grossAmount` and `netAmount`; this will be done in a later exercise. In this program, just assign 0.0 to each of those variables.

To permit the method `inputData` to read and return an employee name, change the type of the variable `employeeName` from class `String` to class `StringBuffer`; you will have to change the type of the corresponding method parameter in `printEmployeeInfo`, as well.

The method `inputData` also needs to read and return values for hourly rate, hours worked, and tax rate. To make this possible, change the types of the variables `hourlyRate`, `hoursWorked`, and `taxRate` from the primitive type `double` to the class `DoubleClass`, found with your Chapter 7 student files. Defined in the class is a constructor with no parameters that is used to initialize the objects instantiated to 0.0. The method `setNum()` is used to set the data member of the object using the method's parameter. The method `getNum()` is used to retrieve the `double` value stored within the object.

Following is a copy of the screen results that should appear after running your program.

```
           Instructions for Payroll Report Program
This program calculates a paycheck for each employee.
A text file containing the following information will be created:
name, pay rate, hours worked, and tax percentage to be deducted.

The program will create a report in columnar format showing the
employee name, hourly rate, number of hours worked, tax rate,
gross pay, and net pay.

After all employees are processed, totals will be displayed,
including total gross amount and total net pay.
```

```
                        Payroll Report
```

Employee Name	Hourly Rate	Hours Worked	Tax Rate	Gross Amount	Net Amount	
--------------------	--------	--------	--------	--------	--------	
John Smith	9.45	40.00	15.00	0.00	0.00	
Jane Doe	12.50	45.00	15.00	0.00	0.00	OT
Harry Morgan	20.00	40.00	20.00	0.00	0.00	
Carmen Martinez	25.00	35.00	25.00	0.00	0.00	
Jacintha Washington	50.85	60.00	34.00	0.00	0.00	OT

Be sure to include comments and display the results to the user.

Write your design in the following space. Your design should be a list of Java comments without any code.

2. b. Write a Java program based on the design you created in Exercise 2a. Save the program as
Payroll3.java to the device or location specified by your instructor. Compile, run, and test the
program. Copy the instructions, input, and output that are displayed, and paste them in a block
comment at the end of your program.

LAB 7.7 IDENTIFYING THE SCOPE OF AN IDENTIFIER

The scope of an identifier refers to that part of a program in which the identifier is accessible. The scope of an identifier defined within a class is limited to the methods of that class. (Static methods are an exception; they cannot access nonstatic identifiers within the same class.)

The scope of an identifier declared within a code block extends from the statement in which it is declared to the end of the block. When one code block is nested within another, an identifier declared in the outer block is accessible within the inner block. (If the inner block declares an identifier of the same name, then it cannot access the identifier in the outer block.)

The scope of a variable declared in a `for` statement is the `for` statement and the body of the `for` loop.

Objectives

In this lab, you learn to recognize the difference between local and global variables and the scope of their identifiers.

After completing this lab, you will be able to:

- Use value parameters and reference variables in the same method.

Identifying the Scope of an Identifier

In the following exercises, you design and write methods for the payroll program.

1. a. In this lab, you continue the stepwise refinement of the payroll program. In the payroll program, design new methods `processPay` and `totalAmounts`. Now, the variables `hourlyRate`, `hoursWorked`, `taxRate`, `grossAmount`, and `netAmount` are to be declared as reference variables of class `DoubleClass`. However, you will use both primitive parameters and reference variables when passing values to the `processPay` method. You also might need to change your call to `printEmployeeInfo` in the method `main`. The `void` method `totalAmounts` uses the class `double` and variables `totalGrossAmount` and `totalNetAmount` that have been declared before `main`.

    You will make the final enhancements to your payroll program. Change the declarations of the variables `grossAmount` and `netAmount` so that they are reference variables of the class `DoubleClass`. Design two new methods, `processPay` (which calculates the gross and net pay amounts) and `totalAmounts` (which prints the gross and net pay amounts). The method `processPay` is called from the loop found in the method `main`, just before the method `printEmployeeInfo` is called. The method `totalAmounts` is called after the loop terminates. You might also need to alter your call to `printEmployeeInfo` in the method `main`.

    The method `processPay` is a `void` method that has five formal parameters: `hourlyRate`, `hoursWorked`, `taxAmount`, `grossAmount`, and `netAmount`. The method calculates `grossAmount` by multiplying `hoursWorked` and `hourlyRate`. If the employee worked overtime (that is, if `hoursWorked` is greater than the constant `FULL_TIME`), then they must be paid time-and-a-half for the hours worked in excess of `FULL_TIME`; in this case, add to `grossAmount` the value obtained by multiplying `hoursWorked` in excess of `FULL_TIME`, `hourlyRate`, and 0.5. To find the value of `netAmount`, multiply `grossAmount` by `taxRate` divided by 100, and then subtract this product from `grossAmount`. Because the method changes the values of the parameters `grossAmount` and `netAmount`, these parameters should be of the class `DoubleClass`; the other parameters should be of the primitive type `double`.

    The method `totalAmounts` prints a label "Total" and the values of the data members `grossAmount` and `netAmount` under the corresponding columns of data.

Be sure to include comments and display the results to the user.

Following is a copy of the screen results that might appear after running your program.

```
             Instructions for Payroll Report Program
This program calculates a paycheck for each employee.
A text file containing the following information will be created:
name, pay rate, hours worked, and tax percentage to be deducted.

The program will create a report in columnar format showing the
employee name, hourly rate, number of hours worked, tax rate,
gross pay, and net pay.

After all employees are processed, totals will be displayed,
including total gross amount and total net pay.
```

```
                          Payroll Report


Employee              Hourly    Hours     Tax      Gross       Net
Name                    Rate   Worked     Rate    Amount    Amount
--------------------  -------- -------- -------- --------  --------
John Smith               9.45    40.00    15.00    378.00    321.30
Jane Doe                12.50    45.00    15.00    593.75    504.69  OT
Harry Morgan            20.00    40.00    20.00    800.00    640.00
Carmen Martinez         25.00    35.00    25.00    875.00    656.25
Jacintha Washington     50.85    60.00    34.00   3559.50   2349.27  OT
Total                                             6206.25   4471.51
```

Write your design in the following space. Your design should be a list of Java comments without any code.

1. b. Write a Java program based on the design you created in Exercise 1a. Save the program as
Payroll4.java to the device or location specified by your instructor. Compile, run, and test the
program. Copy the instructions, input, and output that are displayed, and paste them in a block
comment at the end of your program.

LAB 7.8 USING METHOD OVERLOADING

In a Java program, two or more methods of the same class can have identical names, but such methods must have different signatures. The *signature* of a method is determined by the number, types, and order of its formal parameters. (The return type is not part of the method signature, and does not help distinguish the method from others with matching names.) Defining multiple methods of the same name within a class is known as *method overloading*.

Objectives

In this lab, you use method overloading according to the type of data being processed.

After completing this lab, you will be able to:

- Write methods of the same name with different formal parameter lists.

- Understand method overloading.

Using Method Overloading

In the following exercises, you design and write Java programs that use method overloading.

1. a. Design a program that has five definitions of the method `dataOut`, with each one having a different signature. The signatures for the five method definitions are:

- `char, String, int, double`

- `String, int, double, char`

- `int, double`

- `char, String`

- `char, int`

Within the `method` main, call each `dataOut` method using an appropriate list of arguments chosen from four variables that are declared in `main`:

- A `char` variable named `letter`, assigned the value 'a'

- A `String` variable named `name`, assigned the value "Hello"

- An `int` variable named `number`, assigned the value 5

- A `double` variable named `value`, assigned the value 6.25

Be sure to include comments and display the results to the user.

Following is a copy of the screen results that might appear after running your program.

```
You called dataOut with
  the character a,
  the string Hello,
  the integer number 5,
  and the double number 6.25

You called dataOut with
  the string Hello,
  the integer number 5,
  the double number 6.25,
  and the character a
```

```
You called dataOut with
  the integer number 5
  and the double number 6.25

You called dataOut with
  the character a
  and the string Hello

You called dataOut with
  the character a
  and the integer number 5
```

Write your design in the following space. Your design should be a list of Java comments without any code.

1. b.   Write a Java program based on the design you created in Exercise 1a. Save the program as **PrintData.java** to the device or location specified by your instructor. Compile, run, and test the program. Copy the instructions and output that are displayed, and paste them in a block comment at the end of your program.

8

USER-DEFINED CLASSES AND ADTS

In this chapter, you will:

♦ Learn about user-defined classes

♦ Learn about `private`, `protected`, `public`, and `static` members of a class

♦ Explore how classes are implemented

♦ Learn about the various operations on classes

♦ Examine constructors

♦ Examine the method `toString`

♦ Become aware of accessor and mutator methods

♦ Learn how to create your own packages

♦ Become aware of the reference `this`

♦ Learn about abstract data types (ADTs)

CHAPTER 8: ASSIGNMENT COVER SHEET

Name _____   Date _____

Section _____

Lab Assignments	Grade
Lab 8.1 Defining Classes Using the Unified Modeling Language (UML) Notation	
Lab 8.2 Defining a Class That Creates an Instance of Another Class and Constructors with Parameters	
Lab 8.3 Accessing Class Members Through Objects of the Class (Critical Thinking Exercises)	
Lab 8.4 The Method toString and the Reference this	
Lab 8.5 Using the Abstract Data Type and Information Hiding (Critical Thinking Exercises)	
Total Grade	

See your instructor or the introduction to this book for instructions on submitting your assignments.

LAB 8.1 DEFINING CLASSES USING THE UNIFIED MODELING LANGUAGE (UML) NOTATION

The first step in solving problems with *object-oriented design* (OOD) is to identify the objects that make up the problem domain. An object represents some thing that can be described by a noun; examples include tangible objects such as a telephone or a book, and less tangible objects such as a government or a holiday. An object combines *data* (descriptive attributes such as weight or manufacturer) and *operations* (behaviors or abilities) into one unit. A *class* is a collection of objects that share the same data attributes and behavior; those objects are said to be *instances* of their class. Though all objects of a class share the same data attributes, each has its own *state*, or values of the data attributes. Following is the general syntax for defining a class in Java:

```
modifier(s) class ClassIdentifier modifier(s)
{
    classMembers
}
```

In this syntax, *modifier(s)* are used to alter the behavior of the class, and *classMembers* usually consist of named constants and variable declarations (data attributes) and methods (behaviors).

The nonstatic member variables of a class (that is, those declared without the `static` modifier) are called its *instance variables* because each object of the class (that is, each instance of the class) has its own copy of the members. Nonstatic member variables are allocated at the same time that their object is created. On the other hand, static member variables are called *class variables* because only one copy of each variable is created and shared by all objects of the class. Static data members are allocated at compile time.

In a similar fashion, methods can be declared without or with the `static` modifier, and they are called *instance methods* and *class methods*, respectively. Instance methods can access both instance variables and class variables, but class methods can access only the class variables.

One of the characteristics of the members of a class (variables, methods, and constants) is their visibility. There are four categories of member *visibility*: public, protected, default, and private. *Public* members are declared using the keyword `public`, and they are accessible by any method in any class. *Protected* members are declared using the keyword `protected`, and they will be discussed in a later chapter. *Default* members are declared without any visibility keyword, and they are accessible by any method in any class of the same package; default visibility will be discussed later in this chapter. *Private* members are declared using the keyword `private`, and they are accessible only by methods of the same class.

In addition, every class has a constructor (and, perhaps, more than one). A *default constructor* is a constructor that has no parameters; if you write no constructors for a class, Java provides one for you. This *system-defined default constructor* initializes instance variables to their default values.

A Java program can consist of one or more classes. The controlling class of an application program (that is, the class in which execution begins) must have a `main` method. For example, if you execute a Java program by entering a command such as this:

```
java PriceCalc
```

then the class `PriceCalc` must contain a `main` method.

A class and its members can be described graphically using *Unified Modeling Language* (UML) notation. The UML notation is composed of several diagram types that represent different aspects or views of a solution. One of these is a UML *class diagram*, made up of three boxes stacked vertically. The top box contains the name of the class; the middle box contains the data members and their data types; and the bottom box contains the method names, parameter lists, and return types. A + (plus) sign preceding a data member or method indicates that it is a public member; a − (minus) sign indicates that it is a private member. The # (pound) symbol indicates that it is a protected member.

Objectives

In this lab, you define a class with a default constructor.

After completing this lab, you will be able to:

- Use UML notation.

- Write class definitions.

- Write default constructors.

- Access class members (that is, class variables and class methods) from methods of the class.

Estimated completion time: **50–60 minutes**

Defining Classes and Declaring Objects Using the Unified Modeling Language (UML) Notation

In the following exercises, you create UML diagrams, design classes using your UML diagrams, and code the classes from your designs.

1. a.   Create a UML class diagram for a class named **MyDate** that contains data members and a constructor that meets the criteria in the following list.

- The nonstatic integer data members named **month**, **day**, and **year** should be private members so that they cannot be directly manipulated outside of the class.

- The nonstatic Boolean data member named **good** should be a public member so that it can be accessed outside of the class.

- The constructor **MyDate()** should assign to the member variables the values 1 to **month**, 1 to **day**, 2008 to **year**, and the value **true** to **good**.

1. b.   Use your UML class diagram to design a class called **MyDate**. Your design should be a list of Java comments without any code.

1. c.   Write the Java class **MyDate** based on the UML class diagram and the design you created in Exercises 1a and 1b. Enter your class, name the file **MyDate.java**, and save the file to the device or location specified by your instructor. Compile your class to be used later. (You cannot run your class code now because you have not written a program to test the operations of the class **MyDate**.)

2. a.   Create a UML class diagram for a class named **Money** that contains data members, but no methods. This class is used to identify the type of currency by a character code and amount. The nonstatic **char** data member named **currencyType** and a **double** data member named **currencyAmount** should be public members so that they can be accessed outside of the class.

2. b.   Use your UML class diagram to design a class called **Money**. Your design should be a list of Java comments without any code.

2. c. Write the Java class named Money based on the UML class diagram and the design you created in Exercises 2a and 2b. Enter your class, name the file **Money.java**, and save the file to the device or location specified by your instructor. Compile your class to be used later. (You cannot run your class code now because you have not written a program to test the operations of the class Money.)

Lab 8.2 Defining a Class That Creates an Instance of Another Class and Constructors with Parameters

After you have defined a class, you can declare reference variables and create objects of that type. When you create an object using the **new** operator, a constructor is called automatically for the new object. The choice of constructor called depends on the signature used with the **new** operator and the signatures of the constructors. If the types of the arguments do not match exactly the formal parameters of a constructor, Java uses type conversion to look for the best match. If no match can be found, you receive a compile-time error. The parameter values are used within the constructor to initialize the instance variables.

One special type of constructor is the copy constructor. A *copy constructor* is one that has exactly one parameter—an object of the same class—and copies the data members of the parametric object into the data members of the newly created object.

To access an instance variable or instance method of your class from a method in another class, you use a reference to the object (or a variable that references the object) and the name of the member you want to access. The syntax to accomplish this is the reference, followed by the *dot operator* (also known as the *member access operator*), and then the member name.

Objectives

In this lab, you use a class in a driver program.

After completing this lab, you will be able to:

- Write a class with instance variable fields of a user-defined class.

- Write constructors with parameters.

- Write a copy constructor.

Estimated completion time: **50–60 minutes**

Defining a Class That Creates an Instance of Another Class and Constructors with Parameters

In the following exercises, you update your UML diagram and change the design and code of your programs.

1. a.   Update your UML class diagram for the class **MyDate** and call the new class **MyDate2**. Add a constructor with parameters for month, day, and year that will be used to assign values to the instance variables. Add a method **printDate()** to display the date. You also need a method to validate the date. In programming, *validation* means that the values are checked to ensure that they are valid for their intended use. For example, a month value must be in the range of 1 to 12, inclusive. It does not mean that the data is correct, only valid.

   The UML diagram should meet the following criteria:

   - The constructor **MyDate2(int, int, int)** is passed three integer values as parameters; assigns these values to the integer data members **month**, **day**, and **year**; and assigns the value **false** to **good**. The constructor calls the method **validate()** to make sure that the instance variables contain valid values.

   - The constructor **MyDate2(MyDate2)** assigns the values of the **month**, **day**, **year**, and **good** data members from the parameter to the corresponding data members of the new **MyDate2** object.

- The method named `printDate()` is **void**, has no formal parameters, and is a public member so that it can be accessed outside of the class. The member method `printDate()` displays the date in the format *dd Mmm yyyy*, where *dd* is the two-digit day-of-month, *Mmm* is the first three letters of the month name with the first letter capitalized, and *yyyy* is the four-digit year.

- The method named `validate()` is **void**, has no formal parameters, and is a private member so that it can be accessed only within the class. The method `validate()` checks to make sure that the values for `month` are in the range of 1 to 12, inclusive, the values for `day` are within the range for the appropriate month, and the value for `year` is greater than or equal to 1950. The method `validate()` either displays the message "You entered a valid date" and then calls the method `printDate()`, or it displays the message "You entered an invalid date".

1. b. Design the class `MyDate2`, based on your UML class diagram from Exercise 1a. Your design should be a list of Java comments without any code.

1. c. Write in Java the class **MyDate2**, based on the new UML class diagram and the new design you created in Exercises 1a and 1b. Make a copy of the file MyDate.java and call it **MyDate2.java**; save the copy to the device or location specified by your instructor, and then update the code in MyDate2.java to reflect the new UML diagram and design. Compile your class to be used later.

2. a. *Critical Thinking Exercise*: Create a UML class diagram for a class named **Exchange** that contains data members and member methods that meet the criteria in the following list. This class is used to input, validate, and convert Mexican pesos, Euro dollars, and Swiss francs to U. S. dollars.

- Create instance variables named **sum** and **starting**. These variables are of the **Money** data type that you defined in Lab 8.1. These data members are private members so that they cannot be directly manipulated outside of the class. The data member **starting** contains the starting currency amount and type of currency. The data member **sum** contains the amount converted into U. S. dollars. Remember to use the **new** operator when creating objects.

- The nonstatic Boolean data member named **more** is a public member so that it can be accessed outside of the class. This data member has the value **true** or **false** to indicate whether the user wants to continue processing.

- The **void** method **setAmount()** has no formal parameters and is a private method. The method asks the user to enter the starting amount of money. If the user does not enter a positive value, the method should loop until a positive value is entered.

- The **void** method **setType()** has no formal parameters and is a private method. The method asks the user to enter the type of money—d for U.S. dollars, p for Mexican pesos, f for Swiss francs, e for Euro dollars, or q to quit. If the user does not enter a valid type, the method loops until a valid type is entered. If the user enters 'd,' 'p,' 'f,' or 'e,' the method **setAmount()** is called. If the user enters 'q,' the data member **more** is set to **false** to allow the user to quit.

- The **void** method **convert()** has no formal parameters and is a private method. The method calculates the U. S. dollar equivalent of the variable **starting.currencyAmount** and assigns that value to the variable **sum.currencyAmount**. Use the following exchange rates for your calculation:

    1 dollar = 1.4054 Swiss francs

    1 dollar = 0.9553 Euro dollars

    1 dollar = 9.815 Mexican pesos

- The **void** method **outputType( )** has no formal parameters and is a private method. The method outputs a string representation of the name associated with the **currencyType**. This string will be part of another output message and needs to begin and end with a blank character. Use the following messages:

  If **currencyType** is 'd,' output the string " U. S. dollars ".

  If **currencyType** is 'p,' output the string " Mexican pesos ".

  If **currencyType** is 'e,' output the string " Euro dollars ".

  If **currencyType** is 'f,' output the string " Swiss francs ".

- The **void** method **displayStart( )** has no formal parameters and is a private method. The method displays a message based on the value of the variable **starting.currencyType**. The string is formatted as follows:

  You're starting with *amount* **in** *currency type*

  In this output, *amount* is the starting amount entered by the user and *currency type* is either U. S. dollars, Euro dollars, Swiss francs, or Mexican pesos.

- The Boolean method **setData( )** has no formal parameters and is a public member. The method calls the method **setType( )**. If the data member **more** is **true** and the value of the variable **starting.currencyType** is not equal to 'd,' the method **convert( )** is called. If the data member **more** is **true**, the method **displayStart( )** is called. The method returns the value of the data member **more**.

- The default constructor **Exchange( )** initializes the Boolean data member **more** to **true** and calls the method **setData( )** to initialize the starting currency amount and the starting currency type. The method **setData( )** returns a Boolean value, so you must declare a local variable **temp** in the constructor **Exchange( )** and assign to **temp** the value returned from the call to **setData( )**.

2. b. Design a class named **Exchange** based on your UML class diagram. Your design should be a list of Java comments without any code.

2. c. Write the Java class named **Exchange**, based on the UML diagram and the design you created in Exercises 2a and 2b. Enter your class, name the file **Exchange.java**, and save the file to the device or location specified by your instructor. Compile your class to be used later.

LAB 8.3 ACCESSING CLASS MEMBERS THROUGH OBJECTS OF THE CLASS

To allocate memory for the instance variables of a class, you must create an object of the class using the operator **new**. The general syntax for using the operator **new** follows:

```
new className()
```

or

```
new className(argument1, argument2, ..., argumentN)
```

The class allows you to perform built-in operations on data members within the class. You cannot perform arithmetic operations on objects. If you use relational operators to compare two objects, you are comparing their references (that is, you are comparing their locations within memory).

Objectives

In this lab, you use a class in a driver program.

After completing this lab, you will be able to:

- Instantiate an object of a class.

- Access public class members through objects of the class.

- Access class members from member methods of the class.

Estimated completion time: **50–60 minutes**

Accessing Class Members Through Objects of the Class

In the following exercises, you design and create a driver program.

1. a. Design a driver program that uses the **MyDate2** class you created in Lab 8.2. The driver program is designed to test your **MyDate2** class. The **main** method of your driver program prompts the user with the message "Please enter today's date (month, day, and year separated by spaces):". Declare a local variable named **today** that is of type **MyDate2**, and assign to it a new object created using the input values as arguments to the **MyDate2** constructor. Write your design in the following space as a list of Java comments without any code.

1. b.   Write a Java program based on the design you created in Exercise 1a. For readability, insert blank lines to separate parts of the program. Include comments to explain the different sections of code.

Save the program as **AssnDate.java** to the device or location specified by your instructor. Compile, execute, and test the program with several sets of data to test your class.

Following is a copy of the screen results that might appear after running your program three times, depending on the data entered. The input entered by the user appears in bold.

```
This program is a date validator.
When you enter a date, it will tell you
whether the date is a valid date.  You must enter
a year greater than or equal to 1950.

Please enter today's date (month, day, and year, separated by spaces):
11 23 2005
You entered a valid date 23 Nov 2005


This program is a date validator.
When you enter a date, it will tell you
whether the date is a valid date.  You must enter
a year greater than or equal to 1950.

Please enter today's date (month, day, and year separated by spaces):
2 31 2004
You entered an invalid date


This program is a date validator.
When you enter a date, it will tell you
whether the date is a valid date.  You must enter
a year greater than or equal to 1950.

Please enter today's date (month, day, and year separated by spaces):
13 23 2006
You entered an invalid date
```

2. a. *Critical Thinking Exercise:* Design a driver program that uses the **Exchange** class you created in Lab 8.2. After creating an object of the **Exchange** class, test to see whether the user chose to quit by testing its instance variable **more**. If the user chose to quit, display the message "You quit the program before entering any data." Write a loop that is executed as long as the value of the instance variable **more** is **true**. Call the **Exchange** class method **setData( )** until the user chooses to quit. Write your design in the space provided as a list of Java comments without any code.

2. b. Write a Java program based on the design you created in Exercise 2a. For readability, insert blank lines to separate parts of the program. Include comments to explain the different sections of code.

Save the program as **MoneyEx.java** to the device or location specified by your instructor. Compile, execute, and test the program with several sets of data to test your class. Choose to quit as the first entry for your first run. Then run the program again, making different selections.

Following is a copy of the screen results that might appear, depending on the data entered. The input entered by the user appears in bold.

If the user enters q for the first selection, the program displays the following messages:

```
This is a money changer program.
If you enter the type of money,
(d) for U. S. dollars, (p) for Mexican pesos,
(f) for Swiss francs, (e) for Euro dollars,
or (q) to quit, I will tell you the value
in U. S. dollars.
```

```
Enter type of money (d) for U.S. dollars, (p) for Mexican pesos,
(f)for Swiss francs, (e) for Euro dollars or (q)uit: q
You quit the program before entering any data.
```

If the program is run again and q is not the first selection, the following messages should be displayed:

```
This is a money changer program.
If you enter the type of money,
(d) for U. S. dollars, (p) for Mexican pesos,
(f) for Swiss francs, (e) for Euro dollars,
or (q) to quit, I will tell you the value
in U. S. dollars.

Enter type of money (d) for U.S. dollars, (p) for Mexican pesos,
(f) for Swiss francs, (e) for Euro dollars or (q)uit: d
Starting amount: 1000
You're starting with 1000 in U. S. dollars.

Enter type of money (d) for U.S. dollars, (p) for Mexican pesos,
(f) for Swiss francs, (e) for Euro dollars or (q)uit: p
Starting amount: 103.94
Your starting amount of 103.94 in Mexican pesos is 10.59 in U. S. dollars.

Enter type of money (d) for U.S. dollars, (p) for Mexican pesos,
(f) for Swiss francs, (e) for Euro dollars or (q)uit: f
Starting amount: 73.46
Your starting amount of 73.46 in Swiss francs is 52.27 in U. S. dollars.

Enter type of money (d) for U.S. dollars, (p) for Mexican pesos,
(f) for Swiss francs, (e) for Euro dollars or (q)uit: e
Starting amount: 459
Your starting amount of 459 in Euro dollars is 480.48 in U. S. dollars.

Enter type of money (d) for U.S. dollars, (p) for Mexican pesos,
(f) for Swiss francs, (e) for Euro dollars or (q)uit: q
```

Lab 8.4 The Method toString and the Reference this

In Java, every class is a subclass (directly or indirectly) of the class `Object`. As such, the methods of the class `Object` are inherited by all classes. The method `toString()` is a method of the class `Object` that is used to convert an object to a `String` object. The method `toString()` is public, does not take any parameters, and returns a `String` object. You can override the inherited definition of any method in a class by defining another method of the same name in that class. The definition of the new method will then be called instead of the inherited method.

The method `toString()` can be called explicitly or implicitly. For example, here is an explicit call for an object reference variable `myObj`:

```
String result = "The object is " + myObj.toString();
```

And here is an implicit call for the same object:

```
String result = "The answer is " + myObj;
```

Anytime you use an object or object reference where a `String` object is expected, Java will call the `toString()` method for the object.

Every nonstatic method has an implicitly declared reference variable named `this`, which points to the object for which the method was called. Within the method, data members and methods of the object can be accessed by implicitly or explicitly specifying the object. For example, assume that you have called a method of the class `MyDate2`. In that method, you can implicitly access the data member `year`:

```
System.out.println(year);
```

Or, you can explicitly access the data member:

```
System.out.println(this.year);
```

Sometimes, you might need to refer to the object as a whole; this is achieved simply by using the name `this`.

Objectives

In this lab, you define a method `toString()` to override the default `toString()` method (that is, the one inherited from the class `Object`).

After completing this lab, you will be able to:

- Write a method to override the `toString()` default method.

- Modify a method to use the reference `this`.

Estimated completion time: **15–20 minutes**

Overriding the Default Method toString

In the following exercises, you update your UML diagram and class design, and then revise the `MyDate2` class.

1. a. Update the UML diagram you created for your class `MyDate2`, renaming the class to `MyDatets`. Replace the `printDate()` method with a `toString()` method.

   The method `toString()` has no formal parameters, returns a `String` object, and should be a public member so that it can be accessed outside of the class.

1. b.   Update the design of your class **MyDate2** based on the changes in your UML diagram of **MyDatets**. Your design should be a list of Java comments without any code.

1. c.   Write the class **MyDatets** based on the changes in your UML diagram and design in Exercises 1a and 1b. Make a copy of the file Mydate2.java and call it **MyDatets.java**; save the copy to the device or location specified by your instructor; and then update the code in MyDatets.java to reflect the new UML diagram and design. Modify the method **validate()** to print valid dates by calling **toString()** implicitly using the reference **this**. Compile your class.

1. d.   Make a copy of the file AssnDate.java and call it **AssnDatets.java**; save the copy to the device or location specified by your instructor; then update your AssnDatets.java program to use a **MyDatets** reference variable and object rather than a **MyDate2** reference variable and object, and add a statement to call the **println()** method with only the **MyDatets** object. Compile, execute, and test the program.

Following is a copy of the screen results that might appear after running your program several times, depending on the data entered. The input entered by the user appears in bold.

```
This program is a date validator.
When you enter a date, it will tell you
whether the date is a valid date. You must enter
a year greater than or equal to 1950.

Please enter today's date (month, day, and year separated by spaces):
11 23 2005
You entered a valid date 23 Nov 2005

23 Nov 2005
```

LAB 8.5 USING THE ABSTRACT DATA TYPE AND INFORMATION HIDING

Abstraction is the idea of describing something without considering unwarranted or unwanted detail. In program design, you use abstraction in the form of abstract data types to specify only those aspects of a class that are important to the design. An *abstract data type (ADT)* is one that describes the data and operations of a class without giving implementation details. This concept of hiding the unneeded detail of a class from other classes is also known as *information hiding*.

As we saw earlier, the data members of a class can be divided into two categories: instance variables (nonstatic data members created and stored in each instance of the class), and class variables (static data members created and stored with the class, and shared by the instances of the class).

A method that provides access to the value of a private data member is called an *accessor method*. Many times, the name of such a method begins with "get" (for example, `getAmount`); for this reason, accessor methods are sometimes called "get" methods. An accessor method usually has no formal parameters, and the return data type matches the data type of the member variable to which the method provides access.

A method that permits the value of one or more private data members to be changed by methods outside its class is called a *mutator method*. Many times, the name of such a method begins with "set" (for example, `setAmount`); for this reason, mutator methods are sometimes called "set" methods. A mutator method usually has a `void` return type and one or more formal parameters, the values of which are used to modify the private data members.

Objectives

In this lab, you create your own abstract data type using classes.

After completing this lab, you will be able to:

- Write a program using an abstract data type with static and nonstatic data members.

Estimated completion time: **120–150 minutes**

Using the Abstract Data Type and Information Hiding

In the following exercises, you create a UML diagram for a new program, and then design and write the program.

1. a. *Critical Thinking Exercise:* A traveler wants to purchase a number of traveler's checks, each having a set amount for four different currencies: Mexican pesos, Euro dollars, Swiss francs, and U. S. dollars. The traveler wants to know the value of all traveler's checks in U. S. dollars. When the traveler makes a purchase, he or she withdraws a designated number of traveler's checks of a particular type. Additionally, this transaction should be refused if there are not sufficient traveler's checks of the type designated.

    The traveler can increase the number of traveler's checks by making a deposit, but cannot change the amount of the check after it has been established.

    Create a UML diagram for a class named `Checks` that contains data members and methods that meet the criteria cited in the preceding problem statement.

    Create a class `Checks` that includes the following members:

    - The nonstatic `int` data member named `numberOfChecks` to keep track of the number of traveler's checks available.

    - The nonstatic `int` data member named `faceAmount` to keep track of the face value of the traveler's checks available.

- The nonstatic `char` data member named `countryCode` to keep track of the type of traveler's check being processed.

- The static `double` data member named `balance` to keep track of the total value of all traveler's checks in U. S. dollars.

- The `int` method `getCount( )` to return the number of traveler's checks of a particular type.

- The `int` method `getAmount( )` to return the face value of traveler's checks of a particular type.

- The `double` method `getBalance( )` to return the U. S. dollar amount of all traveler's checks.

- The `void` method `deposit( )` to add or increase the number of traveler's checks of a particular type. The first time a deposit is made, the face amount of the traveler's check is set. The balance is updated to include new deposits of traveler's checks. Each check for a particular kind of currency has the same face value. Purchases can only be made in terms of checks and *not* in terms of amount of currency.

- The `void` method `cashCheck( )` to decrease the number of traveler's checks of a particular type. If no face amount has been set or if there are not enough traveler's checks of a particular type, display a message to the user and do not process the request. The balance is updated to include new withdrawals of traveler's checks.

- The `double` method `convert( )` to convert the deposit or withdrawal amount to U. S. dollars.

1. b. Design a class named `Checks` based on your UML class diagram. Identify in your design those methods that are accessor or mutator methods. Your design should be a list of Java comments without any code.

1. c. Write the class **Checks** based on the UML diagram and the design you created in Exercises 1a and 1b. Enter your class, name the file **Checks.java**, and save the file to the device or location specified by your instructor. Compile your class to be used later.

2. Design a driver program that uses the **Checks** class you implemented in Exercise 1. Your **main** method uses a grid layout, which was introduced in Chapter 6, for the user to select from among the choices of Mexican peso, Swiss franc, Euro dollar, U. S. dollar, Check Balance, or Exit.

   If the user selects a currency type, use an input dialog box to prompt the user to specify either a deposit or withdrawal operation, or to quit.

   When the user selects a deposit of a particular type and the current amount for that type is zero, the user is instructed to enter the number of checks and the face amount of the check to be deposited. Otherwise, the user is asked to enter only the number of checks. The balance of the traveler's checks is updated by the equivalent amount of the deposit in U. S. dollars.

   If the user selects a withdrawal, the user is notified if there has never been a deposit of a particular type. In addition, the user is notified if the number of traveler's checks is not available for the amount requested. The balance of the traveler's checks is updated by the equivalent amount of the deposit in U. S. dollars.

   When the user selects quit, a message box appears to inform the user that the check cashing is complete.

   Save the program as **TravlChk.java** to the device or location specified by your instructor. Compile, execute, and test the program with several sets of data to test your class. Following are copies of the screen results that might appear after running your program:

Figure 8-1   Traveler's Check Machine dialog box

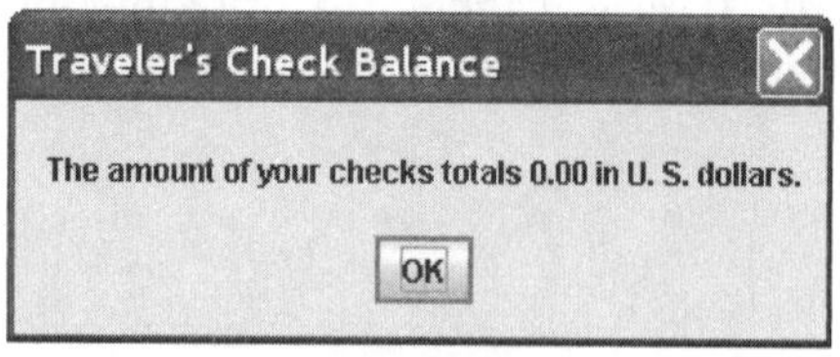

Figure 8-2   Traveler's Check Balance dialog box

Figure 8-3   No Checks Available dialog box

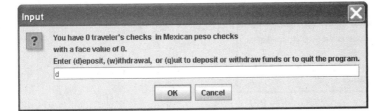

Figure 8-4   Checking the number of Mexican peso checks

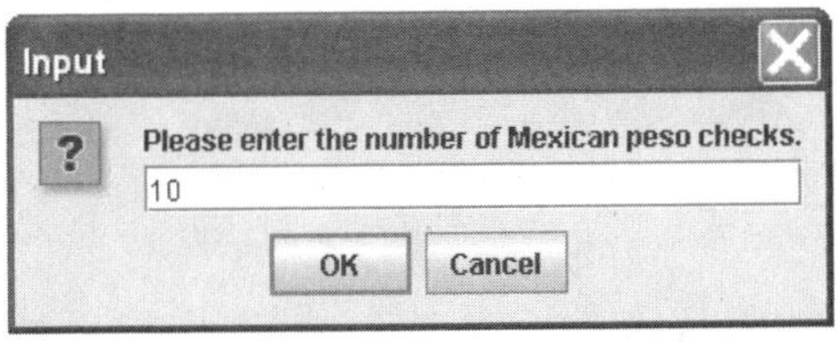

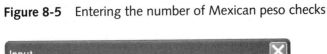

Figure 8-5   Entering the number of Mexican peso checks

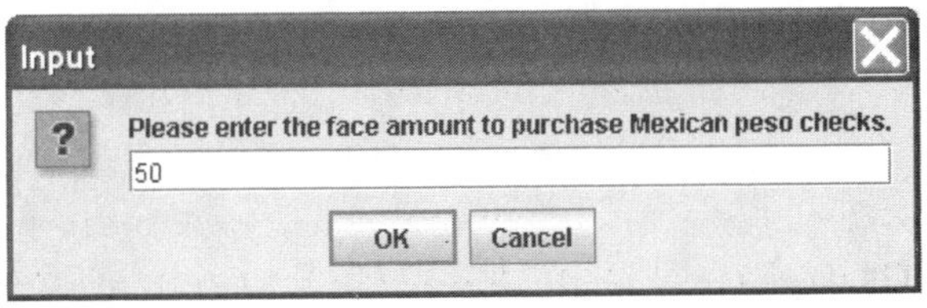

Figure 8-6   Purchasing Mexican peso checks

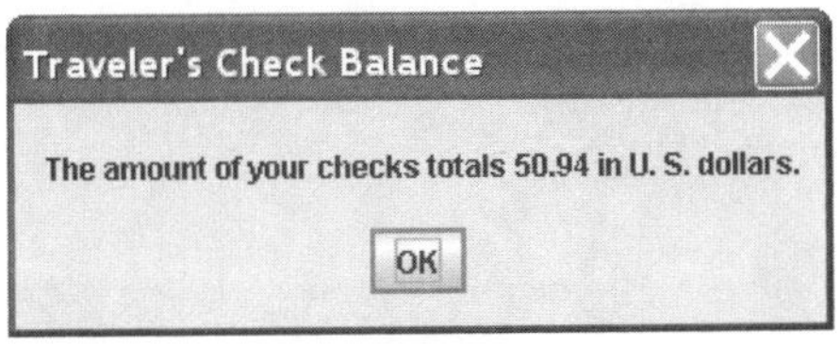

Figure 8-7   Calculating the amount of Mexican peso checks

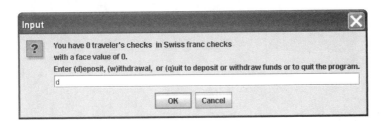

Figure 8-8   Checking the number of Swiss franc checks

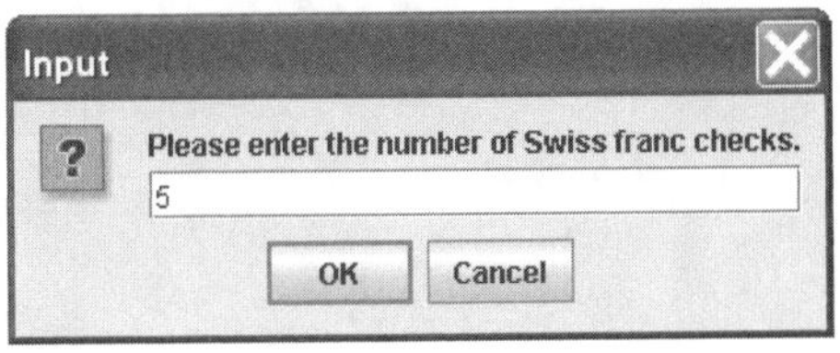

Figure 8-9   Entering the number of Swiss franc checks

Figure 8-10   Purchasing Swiss franc checks

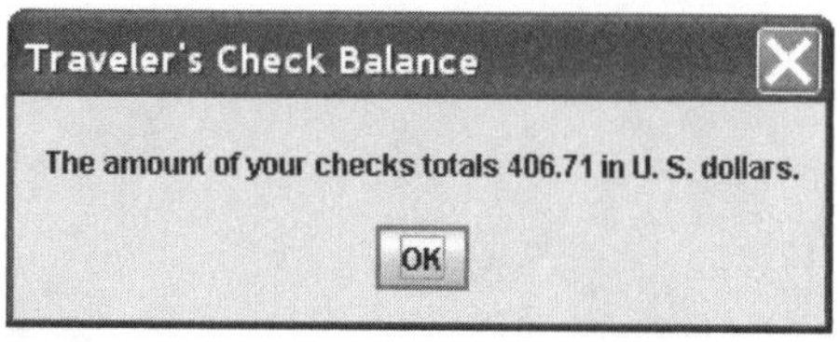

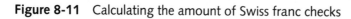

Figure 8-11   Calculating the amount of Swiss franc checks

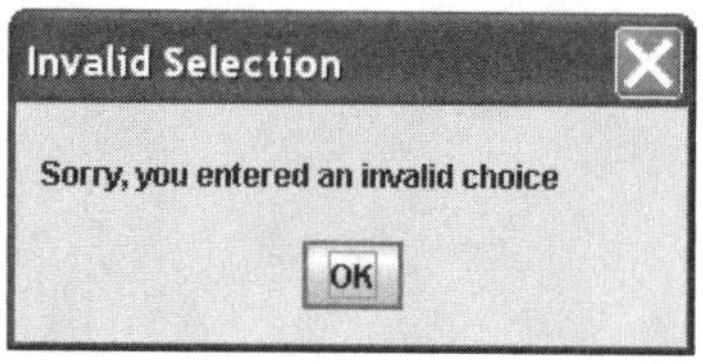

Figure 8-12   The user makes an invalid choice

Either copy the grid and dialog boxes that appear and paste them into a document or print the screens of the grid and dialog boxes.

ARRAYS

In this chapter, you will:

- ◆ Learn about arrays
- ◆ Explore how to declare and manipulate data into arrays
- ◆ Learn about the instance variable `length`
- ◆ Understand the meaning of "array index out of bounds"
- ◆ Become aware of how the assignment and relational operators work with array names
- ◆ Discover how to pass an array as a parameter to a method
- ◆ Discover how to manipulate data in a two-dimensional array
- ◆ Learn about multidimensional arrays

CHAPTER 9: ASSIGNMENT COVER SHEET

Name _____   Date _____

Section _____

Lab Assignments	Grade
Lab 9.1 Declaring and Processing Arrays	
Lab 9.2 Checking Index Bounds and Initializing Arrays	
Lab 9.3 Passing Arrays as Parameters to Methods (Critical Thinking Exercises)	
Lab 9.4 Coding with Parallel Arrays and with an Array of Objects	
Lab 9.5 Manipulating Data in a Two-Dimensional Array and a Multidimensional Array (Critical Thinking Exercises)	
Total Grade	

See your instructor or the introduction to this book for instructions on submitting your assignments.

LAB 9.1 DECLARING AND PROCESSING ARRAYS

An *array* is an object that is a collection of a fixed number of components, called *elements*, wherein all the components are of the same data type. Arrays generally are accessed through reference variables, like other objects. The general syntax to declare a one-dimensional array reference variable is:

```
dataType[] arrayName;
```

Note that Java also accepts the declaration as:

```
dataType arrayName[];
```

but this syntax is not standard.

The general syntax to instantiate an array object is:

```
arrayName = new dataType[intExp];
```

where *intExp* is an integral expression that specifies the number of elements in the array. Java automatically initializes all array elements to their default values at instantiation. Sometimes, array objects are created after program execution begins; such arrays are known as *dynamic arrays*.

The elements of an array are accessed through their position within the array, also known as their *index*. The indices in an array containing *n* elements range from 0 (the index of the first element) through *n*-1 (the index of the last element). To access any given array element, you use an array reference or array variable followed by an integral expression enclosed in square brackets; the value of that expression specifies the index of the element accessed.

Generally, you can use an array element as you would use any variable of the same data type. For example, the following code would assign the value of the variable num to the fourth element in an array:

```
int[] array = new int[5];

int num;

num = array[3];
```

A public instance variable named `length` is associated with each array object, and contains the size of (that is, the number of elements in) the array.

Working with arrays almost always involves iteration.

Objectives

In this lab, you declare, instantiate, and process the elements of an array.

After completing this lab, you will be able to:

- Declare and instantiate a one-dimensional array object.
- Specify an array size during program execution.
- Process a one-dimensional array.
- Access individual array elements.

Estimated completion time: **50–60 minutes**

Declaring and Processing Arrays

In the following exercises, you design and write programs using arrays.

1. a. Design a program that records and reports the weekly sales amounts for the salespeople of a company. Each of the *n* salespeople is assigned a unique identification number in the range of 1 to *n*. The program prompts the user to enter the number of salespeople, and it uses that value to create a dynamic array of sales amounts.

The program then asks the user to enter the ID number and sales amount for each salesperson. The ID numbers in the range of 1 to *n* correspond to the array elements 0 to *n*-1, respectively, so the program should verify that the ID is valid; if not, then the program informs the user and tells him or her to try again.

After a sales amount has been entered for each salesperson, print the sales in a tabular format that displays the ID numbers and sales amounts. The information in the table appears in ascending order, based on ID number.

Following is a copy of the screen results that might appear after running your program, depending on the data entered. The input entered by the user is shown in bold.

```
This is a sales tracking program.
You will enter the number of salespeople, and the
ID number and sales amount for each salesperson.
The sales and total sales will then be displayed.

Please enter the number of salespeople to be processed: 5

Enter an ID number and sales amount separated by a space: 5 340.50
Enter an ID number and sales amount separated by a space: 1 275.75
Enter an ID number and sales amount separated by a space: 2 0
Enter an ID number and sales amount separated by a space: 4 225
Enter an ID number and sales amount separated by a space: 3 175.50

                Weekly Sales by Salesperson

0       1       2       3       4
275.75  0.00    175.50  225.00  340.50
Total Sales:    1016.75
```

Write your design in the following space. Your design should be a list of Java comments without any code.

1. b. Write a Java program based on the design that you created in Exercise 1a. Save the program as **Sales.java** to the device or location specified by your instructor. Compile, run, and test the program. Copy the instructions, input, and output that are displayed, and paste them in a block comment at the end of your program. Then print your program to submit with your work.

Lab 9.2 Checking Index Bounds and Initializing Arrays

An array can be initialized at declaration using a list of values separated by commas; this list is enclosed within braces. The size of the array defaults to the number of values in the initialization list. If an array is declared and initialized at the same time, you do not use the **new** operator to instantiate the array object.

For example, an array with no initialization is defined as follows:

```
dataType[] arrayName;
arrayName = new dataType [intExp];
```

or combined:

```
dataType[] arrayName = new dataType[intExp];
```

An array initialized at declaration is defined as follows:

```
dataType[] arrayName = {value1, value2, value3, ..., valuen};
```

This array is of size *n*.

If an array index goes out of bounds during program execution, it throws an `ArrayIndexOutOfBoundsException` exception. Remember that array variables are accessed with the index values 0 through the size of the array minus one. One common error is to use the array size as an index. For example, the following is an error:

```
int[] array = new int[5];
array[5] = 24;
```

To copy the values of one array into another, you need to copy each value; this usually is accomplished using a loop:

```
int[] arrayA = new int[5];
int[] arrayB = new int[5];
for (int index = 0; index < arrayB.length; index++)
     arrayA[index] = arrayB[index];
```

Objectives

In this lab, you check to see that an index value is in bounds and initialize an array at declaration.

After completing this lab, you will be able to:

- Check for array index out of bounds.

- Initialize arrays at declaration.

Estimated completion time: **40–50 minutes**

Checking Index Bounds and Initializing Arrays

In the following exercises, you design and write a program that initializes an array at declaration and checks array indices to make sure they are in bounds.

1. a. Design a program for a trucking company that has seven trucks in its fleet. Each truck is identified by a unique number from one to seven. Each truck also has a maximum weight allowance, which already has been determined. Assign the maximum weight limit to each truck at initialization. Before a truck can begin its route, it must be weighed to see if it falls within its weight allowance. Ask the user for a truck number and the loaded weight. Display a message indicating whether the truck falls in the allowable weight limit. Do this for each truck. Use the following values as maximum weight limits and enter the weigh-in values for each truck when the program is run:

Truck number	Maximum weight limit	Truck weigh-in
1	50,000	45,000
2	25,000	30,000
3	20,000	20,000
4	35,000	30,000
5	40,000	35,000
6	25,000	27,000
7	30,000	20,000

Following are copies of dialog boxes that might appear after running your program, depending on the data entered.

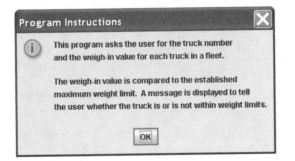

Figure 9-1   Program Instructions dialog box

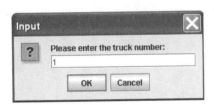

Figure 9-2   Truck Number Input dialog box

Figure 9-3   Truck Weight Input dialog box

Figure 9-4   Truck Within Limits Message dialog box

Figure 9-5   Truck Number Input dialog box

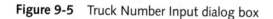

Figure 9-6   Truck Weight Input dialog box

Figure 9-7   Truck Excess Weight Message dialog box

Figure 9-8   Truck Number Input dialog box

Figure 9-9   Truck Weight Input dialog box

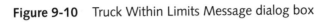

Figure 9-10 Truck Within Limits Message dialog box

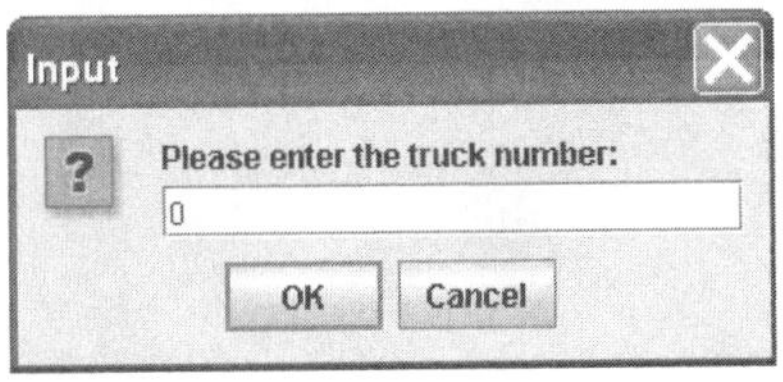

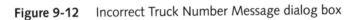

Figure 9-11 Truck Number Input dialog box

Figure 9-12 Incorrect Truck Number Message dialog box

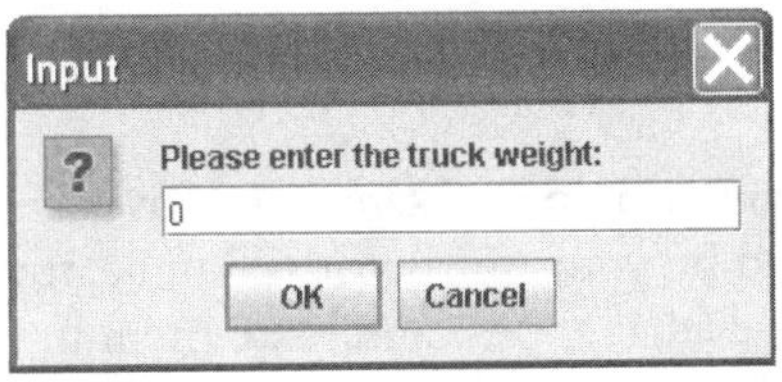

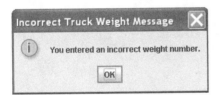

Figure 9-13 Truck Weight Input dialog box

Figure 9-14 Incorrect Truck Weight Message dialog box

Figure 9-15 Truck Weigh-In Complete dialog box

Write your design in the following space. Your design should be a list of Java comments without any code.

1. b. Write a Java program based on the design that you created in Exercise 1a. Save the program as **Trucks.java** to the device or location specified by your instructor. Compile, run, and test the program. Either copy the grid and dialog boxes that appear and paste them into a document or print the screens of the grid and dialog boxes. Then print your program to submit with your work.

LAB 9.3 PASSING ARRAYS AS PARAMETERS TO METHODS

Like other objects, arrays can be passed as parameters to methods. If the number of array elements to be processed by the method is less than the size of the array, then the number of elements to be processed also should be passed to the method.

When the name of an array variable is used by itself (that is, without being followed by an index within square brackets), it represents the memory address of the first element of the array to which the variable refers. This address is known as the *base address* of the array. When you pass an array variable or an array reference as an argument to a method, the base address of the array is passed into the formal parameter.

Objectives

In this lab, you initialize an array at declaration, and use an array as an argument to a method.

After completing this lab, you will be able to:

■ Initialize a Boolean array.

■ Use arrays as arguments to methods.

Estimated completion time: **80–90 minutes**

Passing Arrays as Parameters to Methods

In the following exercises, you design and write a program that passes an array to a method as a parameter.

1. a. *Critical Thinking Exercise*: Design a program to search a word for letters that the user enters. Declare a Boolean array of size 26 to represent each letter of the alphabet. (Remember that the alphabet contains 52 characters if you count uppercase and lowercase, so your program converts all letters entered by the user to the same case.) You do not need to initialize the elements of this array to `false` at declaration, because `false` is the default value when a Boolean array is initialized. If the program finds within the word a letter that the user enters, change the value of the array element that matches the letter by position to `true`.

    Design a method that prompts the user for a letter to be found and returns the response. Design another method that counts the number of occurrences of a letter in a word and returns that count. Design yet another method that displays the letters entered by the user that are also present in the word. These methods are called by the method `main`.

    Following is a copy of the screen results that might appear after running your program, depending on the data entered. The input entered by the user is in bold.

    ```
    This is a program that counts each time a
    letter in the alphabet occurs in a word.

    Please enter a word: howdy
    The word howdy has 5 characters.

    What letter would you like to guess? (Enter zero to quit.) a
    There are 0 A's.

    What letter would you like to guess? (Enter zero to quit.) b
    There are 0 B's.

    What letter would you like to guess? (Enter zero to quit.) c
    There are 0 C's.
    ```

```
What letter would you like to guess? (Enter zero to quit.) d
There are 1 D's.

What letter would you like to guess? (Enter zero to quit.) e
There are 0 E's.

What letter would you like to guess? (Enter zero to quit.) f
There are 0 F's.

What letter would you like to guess? (Enter zero to quit.) g
There are 0 G's.

What letter would you like to guess? (Enter zero to quit.) h
There are 1 H's.

What letter would you like to guess? (Enter zero to quit.) 0
You found these letters:
D
H
```

Write your design in the following space. Your design should be a list of Java comments without any code.

1. b.   Write a Java program based on the design that you created in Exercise 1a. Save the program as **CountLet.java** to the device or location specified by your instructor. Compile, run, and test the program. Copy the instructions, input, and output that are displayed, and paste them in a block comment at the end of your program. Then print your program to submit with your work.

LAB 9.4 CODING WITH PARALLEL ARRAYS AND WITH AN ARRAY OF OBJECTS

Parallel arrays are two or more arrays, the corresponding elements of which hold related information. Generally, you use a parallel array whenever you need to keep track of multiple pieces of information for each component of a collection. For example, a `String` array of student names and a `double` array of their grade point averages could be implemented using parallel arrays.

As an alternative to parallel arrays, you can create a class that contains a data member for each piece of information (such as student name and grade point average), and then create and manipulate an array of these objects. The syntax for declaring an array reference variable and creating an array of objects is:

```
dataType[] reference = new dataType[size];
```

This statement only creates an array of references. Only one object, the array itself, is instantiated from this statement.

Objectives

In this lab, you process parallel arrays and an array of objects.

After completing this lab, you will be able to:

- Process parallel arrays.

- Process an array of objects.

Estimated completion time: **60–90 minutes**

Coding with Parallel Arrays and with an Array of Objects

In the following exercises, you design and write a program that uses parallel arrays. You create a UML class diagram for the program, and you design and write a class based on the UML diagram. Then, you design a driver program that uses the class you wrote.

1. a. Design a program to keep track of the hits, walks, and outs of a baseball team. Use parallel arrays to keep track of each player's accumulated statistics. The player number is the index of the array. Ask the user for the player number, hits, walks, and outs for each game. Enter data for multiple games with nine batters per game. The team has 20 players, but only nine will have statistics for a particular game.

    Display the accumulated hits, walks, and outs for all players for the season.

    Following is a copy of some of the screen results that might appear after running your program, depending on the data entered. The instructions should resemble the following when you use the input given.

    ```
    This program asks the user for a baseball player's number,
    and their number of hits, walks, and outs for multiple games.
    Only nine players bat each game.

    For game 1, enter the player number: 1
    Enter the hits for game 1 for player 1: 2
    Enter the walks for game 1 for player 1: 2
    Enter the outs for game 1 for player 1: 2
    ```

    Test using the following input:

    ```
    1 2 2 2
    20  0 5 1
    2 0 0 6
    18 4 2 0
    ```

```
3  2  1  3
4  1  2  3
7  0  0  3
8  1  4  1
9  3  2  1
10 2  2  2
11 6  0  0
12 2  2  2
2  0  5  1
20 0  0  6
17 4  2  0
4  2  1  3
3  1  2  3
7  0  0  3
```

The output should resemble the following code:

```
Player   Hits    Walks   Outs
------   ----    -----   ----
1        2       2       2
2        0       5       7
3        3       3       6
4        3       3       6
5        0       0       0
6        0       0       0
7        0       0       6
8        1       4       1
9        3       2       1
10       2       2       2
11       6       0       0
12       2       2       2
13       0       0       0
14       0       0       0
15       0       0       0
16       0       0       0
17       4       2       0
18       4       2       0
19       0       0       0
20       0       5       7
```

Write your design in the following space. Your design should be a list of Java comments without any code.

1. b. Write a Java program based on the design that you created in Exercise 1a. Save the program as **Baseball.java** to the device or location specified by your instructor. Compile, run, and test the program. Copy the instructions, input, and output that are displayed, and paste them in a block comment at the end of your program. Then print your program to submit with your work.

2. a. Create a UML diagram for a class named Player that contains data members and three methods that input values for one player in a particular game number, update the statistics for that player using the data, and display the statistics for one player, as described in the Exercise 1a problem statement.

2. b. Design a class named Player based on your UML diagram. Your design should be a list of Java comments without any code.

2. c.   Write a Java class Player based on the UML diagram and the design you created in Exercises 2a and 2b. Enter your class, name it **Player.java**, and save it to the device or location specified by your instructor. Compile your class to be used later.

3. a.   Design a driver program that imports the Player class you implemented in Exercise 2. Ask the user for the number of players on the team, though only nine will have statistics for a particular game. Also ask the user for the number of games in the season.

Use an array of the type Player as defined in Exercise 2. Your array will be the size of the number of players on the team as entered by the user. You will accumulate all the hits, runs, and walks for all games of the season. The user will input the number of games for the season.

Display the accumulated hits, walks, and outs for all players for the season.

Following is a copy of some of the instructions that should appear when running your program.

```
This program tracks a baseball player's number, and their
number of hits, walks, and outs for each game in a season.
Only nine players bat each game.

How many players are on your team? 20
How many games are played this season? 2

For game 1, enter the player number (-1 to quit): 1
Enter the hits for game 1 for player 1: 2
Enter the walks for game 1 for player 1: 2
Enter the outs for game 1 for player 1: 2
```

Write your design in the following space. Your design should be a list of Java comments without any code.

3. b. Write a Java program based on the design that you created in Exercise 3a. Save the program as
Baseball2.java to the device or location specified by your instructor. Compile, run, and test
the program with the same data used in Exercise 1. Copy the instructions, input, and output
that are displayed, and paste them in a block comment at the end of your program. Then print
your program to submit with your work.

LAB 9.5 MANIPULATING DATA IN A TWO-DIMENSIONAL ARRAY AND A MULTIDIMENSIONAL ARRAY

In the previous lab, you manipulated parallel arrays and arrays of objects. Because all data types in the problem are the same, you could manipulate the data in table form by using a two-dimensional array. The syntax for declaring a two-dimensional array is:

```
dataType[][] arrayName;
```

The general syntax to instantiate a two-dimensional array object is:

```
arrayName = new dataType[intExp1][intExp2];
```

The expression *intExp1* specifies the number of rows and the expression *intExp2* specifies the number of columns in the array.

Java allows you to specify a different number of columns for each row, creating what is called a *ragged array*. In this case, each row must be instantiated separately. The syntax is:

```
dataType[][] arrayName;
arrayName = new dataType[rows];   //Create the row references
arrayName[0] = new dataType[cols0];   //Create the 1st row.
arrayName[1] = new dataType[cols1];   //Create the 2nd row.
   ...
arrayName[rows - 1] = new dataType[colsLast];   //Create the last row.
```

A two-dimensional array can be processed in three ways:

1. Process the entire array.

2. Process some rows of the array, called *row processing*.

3. Process some columns of the array, called *column processing*.

A collection of a fixed number of elements arranged in *n* dimensions where *n* is greater than or equal to 1 is called an *n-dimensional array*. The general syntax for declaring and instantiating an n-dimensional array is:

```
dataType[][]...[] arrayName
        = new dataType[intExp1][intExp2]...[intExpn];
```

Objectives

In this lab, you declare, instantiate, and process the components of a multidimensional array.

After completing this lab, you will be able to:

- Declare and instantiate a two-dimensional array object.

- Process a two-dimensional array.

- Process a two-dimensional array by columns.

- Declare and instantiate a three-dimensional array object.

- Process a three-dimensional array.

- Process a three-dimensional array by column and by the third dimension.

Estimated completion time: **120–150 minutes**

Manipulating Data in a Two-Dimensional and a Multidimensional Array

In the following exercises, you use a two-dimensional array instead of parallel arrays to redesign the program you created in Lab 9.4. You also redesign the program to use a three-dimensional array.

1. a. Refer to the program design in Lab 9.4 Exercise 1. Instead of using parallel arrays, use a two-dimensional array to design a program to keep track of baseball players' hits, runs, and outs for a season. Allow the user to determine the number of players on the team and the number of games in the season. Test to be sure that there are at least nine players and one game. Display the total number of hits, walks, and outs of each player and the total of hits, walks, and outs for the team. Test your program for less than nine players, and then test using the same data listed in Lab 9.4 Exercise 1.

Following is a copy of some of the instructions that should appear when running your program and entering fewer than nine players. The input entered by the user is shown in bold.

```
This program asks the user for a baseball player's number,
and their number of hits, walks, and outs for each game in a season.
Only nine players bat each game.

How many players are on the team?  2
You cannot play with less than 9 players!
```

When running your program using the test data from Lab 9.4 Exercise 1, your output should resemble the output shown in Lab 9.4, except for your instructions and total lines.

Following is a copy of some of the instructions that should appear when running your program. The input entered by the user is shown in bold.

```
This program asks the user for a baseball player's number,
and his number of hits, walks, and outs for each game in a season.
Only nine players bat each game.

How many players are on the team?  20
How many games are in the season?  2

For game 1 enter the player number (-1 to quit): 1
Enter the hits for game 1 for player 1: 2
Enter the walks for game 1 for player 1: 2
Enter the outs for game 1 for player 1: 2
```

The total line should resemble:

```
Totals  30      32      40
```

Write your design in the following space. Your design should be a list describing what happens at each line in the program, or should use the format your instructor requires.

1. b. Write a Java program based on the design that you created in Exercise 1a. Save the program as **Baseball3.java** to the device or location specified by your instructor. Compile, run, and test the program. Copy the instructions, input, and output that are displayed, and paste them in a block comment at the end of your program. Then print your program to submit with your work.

2. a. *Critical Thinking Exercise*: Redesign the program you created in Exercise 1a to use a three-dimensional array. Instead of using columns as accumulators for total hits, walks, and outs, the rows should contain the hits, walks, and outs for each game. Your third dimension should represent the game. Display the values for each player who played by game. Do not display any data for a game in which a player did not participate. Display the total number of hits, walks, and outs by game and by season.

The user instructions should be the same as in Exercise 1. Following is a copy of the output that should appear when running your program with the test data from Exercise 1.

Player	Hits	Walks	Outs
------	-----	-----	----
1	2	2	2
2	0	0	6
3	2	1	3
4	1	2	3
7	0	0	3
8	1	4	1
9	3	2	1
18	4	2	0
20	0	5	1

Game 1 Totals

Totals	13	18	20
2	0	5	1
3	1	2	3
4	2	1	3
7	0	0	3
10	2	2	2
11	6	0	0
12	2	2	2
17	4	2	0
20	0	0	6

Game 2 Totals

Totals	17	14	20

Season Totals

Totals	30	32	40

2. b. Write a Java program based on the design that you created in Exercise 2a. Save the program as **Baseball4.java** to the device or location specified by your instructor. Compile, run, and test the program. Copy the instructions, input, and output that are displayed, and paste them in a block comment at the end of your program. Then print your program to submit with your work.

Applications of Arrays (Searching and Sorting) and Strings

In this chapter, you will:

♦ Learn how to implement the sequential search algorithm

♦ Explore how to sort an array using the selection sort algorithm

♦ Learn how to implement the sequential search on a sorted list

♦ Learn how to implement the binary search algorithm

♦ Become acquainted with the class `Vector`

♦ Learn about manipulating strings using the class `String`

CHAPTER 10: ASSIGNMENT COVER SHEET

Name _____   Date _____

Section _____

Lab Assignments	Grade
Lab 10.1 Implementing the Sequential Search Algorithm	
Lab 10.2 Sorting an Array Using Selection Sort	
Lab 10.3 Implementing the Binary Search Algorithm	
Lab 10.4 Using the Class Vector (Critical Thinking Exercises)	
Lab 10.5 Using String Methods (Critical Thinking Exercises)	
Total Grade	

See your instructor or the introduction to this book for instructions on submitting your assignments.

LAB 10.1 IMPLEMENTING THE SEQUENTIAL SEARCH ALGORITHM

Lists can be stored in arrays. You can perform the following basic operations on a list:

- Input a list.
- Output a list.
- Search the list for a given item.
- Sort the list.
- Insert an item in the list.
- Delete an item from the list.

One way to search a list is to determine the item for which you are searching and the length of the list to be searched. After searching a list, you need to know if the item was found. If the item was found, you also usually need to know the array index or a reference to the element where it was found.

Searching the elements of a list, from beginning to end until an item is found, is called a *sequential search* or *linear search*.

Objectives

In this lab, you search a list of a particular size for a given value, and then you indicate whether the item is found. If it is, you also indicate the location where the item was found.

After completing this lab, you will be able to:

- Search a list of a given size for a particular value.
- Report whether the item is found in the list.
- If the item was found, report the location in the list where it was found.

Estimated completion time: **50–60 minutes**

Implementing the Sequential Search Algorithm

In the following exercises, you design and write a program that searches a list for a number and reports where it is found.

1. a. Design a program that simulates a contest for a radio station that awards a $10,000 prize to the first caller who correctly guesses a number in a list of randomly generated numbers. Each caller can make only one guess. The contest is held until a number has been matched or the user enters a value of –1. The following numbers were found using a program to randomly generate 20 numbers. Either assign the following 20 different values between 1 and 500 to an array, or write your own program to randomly generate your numbers.

42
468
335
1
170
225
479
359
463
465
206
146

```
282
329
462
492
496
443
328
437
```

Display a message indicating the winning number, its location in the list of random numbers, the number of calls made, and the amount of the prize.

Following is a copy of some of the screen results that might appear after running your program, depending on the data entered.

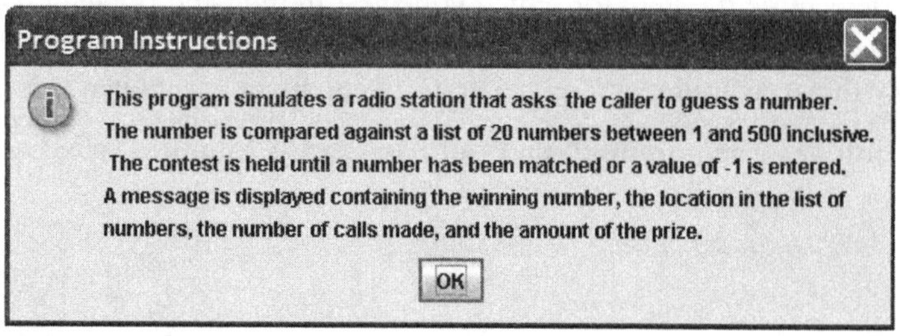

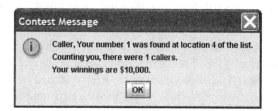

Figure 10-1   Program Instructions dialog box

If the program finds a value on the list with the first guess, the following dialog boxes appear, depending on the data entered:

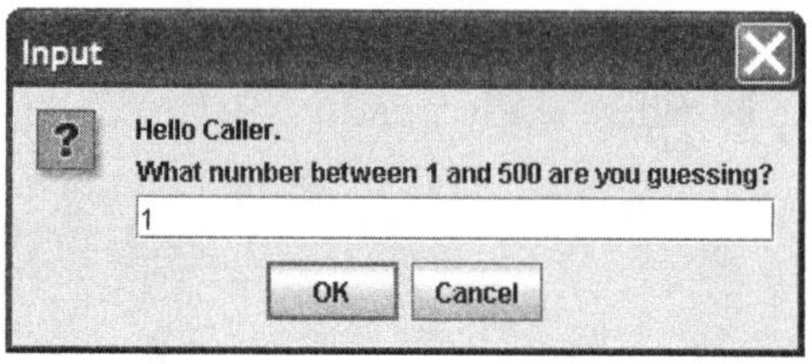

Figure 10-2   Caller Guess Input dialog box

Figure 10-3   Contest Message dialog box

If the user does not immediately enter a value on the list when the program runs, the following additional dialog boxes should appear, depending on the data entered:

Figure 10-4   Guess Not Found Message dialog box

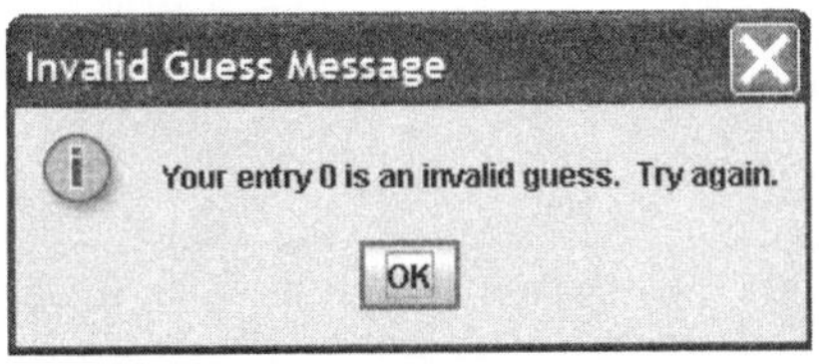

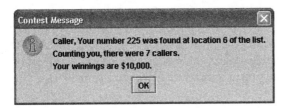

Figure 10-5   Invalid Guess Message dialog box

Figure 10-6   Contest Message dialog box

Write your design in the following space. Your design should be a list of Java comments without any code.

1. b. Write a Java program based on the design that you created in Exercise 1a. Save the program as **Prize.java** to the device or location specified by your instructor. Compile, run, and test the program. Either copy the dialog boxes that appear and paste them into a document or print screens of the dialog boxes. Then print your program to submit with your work.

LAB 10.2 SORTING AN ARRAY USING SELECTION SORT

The *selection sort* algorithm rearranges a list of values by selecting elements one at a time from the list and moving them to their proper position. For example, if you are using selection sort to put the list elements in ascending order, you would first move the smallest value in the list to the first location. Then, you would move the next smallest item to the second location, and so on. You can also put the list elements in descending order by placing the largest value in the first position, the second largest value in the second position, and so on.

A sorted list (also called an *ordered list*) can be searched sequentially more efficiently than can an unsorted list. For example, when you reach a value in an ascending sorted list that is greater than the value for which you are searching, the search can be stopped because the value will not be found. Similarly, when you are searching a descending sorted list, you can stop searching when you reach a value in the list that is smaller than the value for which you are searching.

Objectives

In this lab, you become acquainted with the selection sort. You also search an ordered list of a particular size for a value. Indicate whether the item is found; if it is, indicate the location where the item was found. If the number is not in the search list, discontinue the search when a list value exceeds the search value.

After completing this lab, you will be able to:

- Sort an unordered list using the selection sort.

- Search an ordered list of a given size for a particular value.

- Report if an item is found in the list.

- If the item was found, report the location in the list where it was found.

- If the item was not found, stop the search when a list value exceeds the search value and then indicate that the value was not found.

Estimated completion time: **60–90 minutes**

Sorting an Array Using Selection Sort

In the following exercises, you design and write a program that sorts a list.

1. a. Design a program that sorts the same list of 20 values that you used in Lab 10.1. The design of your `main` method should consist of a list of calls to three methods, where all work is performed. Sort the array using the selection sort algorithm in one method. Write the sorted array to an output file called **prizeNos.srt** in another method and save the file to the device or location specified by your instructor. Output the original list and the sorted list to the screen in a third method. Print the **prizeNos.srt** file and compare the lists.

   Following is a copy of the screen results that might appear after running your program, depending on the data entered.

   ```
   Your beginning list:
   42
   468
   335
   1
   170
   225
   ```

```
479
359
463
465
206
146
282
329
462
492
496
443
328
437
```

```
Your sorted list:
1
42
146
170
206
225
282
328
329
335
359
437
443
462
463
465
468
479
492
496
```

The following list is the contents of the file **prizeNos.srt**:

```
1
42
146
170
206
225
282
328
329
335
359
437
443
462
463
465
468
479
492
496
```

Write your design in the following space. Your design should be a list of Java comments without any code.

1. b. Write a Java program based on the design that you created in Exercise 1a. Save the program as **SortList.java** to the device or location specified by your instructor. Compile, run, and test the program. Copy the instructions and the output that is displayed, and paste them in a block comment at the end of your program. Then print your program to submit with your work.

2. a. Design a program to sequentially search the ordered list found in the file **prizeNos.srt**, created in Exercise 1. Because the list is in ascending order, there are steps you can take to make the search "smarter":

   ■ If the value for which you are searching is less than the value of the first list element or greater than the value of the last list element, then the search value is not in the list.

   ■ If the search value falls within the range of element values, you can begin the search at the first element of the list and stop searching as soon as you reach a list element with a value that is greater than the search value; the search value is not in the list.

   Similar steps can be taken to improve the search when the list is sorted in descending order.

   You should have the same screen results as those in Lab 10.1. You also will have additional output messages, depending on the data entered.

   If the guess is less than the smallest number on the list or greater than the largest number on the list, the following message should be displayed:

   ```
   It took 0 comparisons to check the list.
   ```

   For all other guesses, the program will display the following message:

   ```
   It took n comparisons to check the list.
   ```

   In this message, n is a value between 1 and 20, inclusively.

   Write your design in the following space. Your design should be a list of Java comments without any code.

2. b. Implement the new design in Java. Save the program as **Prize2.java** to the device or location specified by your instructor. Compile, run, and test the program. After executing your program, select and copy everything that appears on your screen. Paste the copied text into a comment block at the end of your program.

Lab 10.3 Implementing the Binary Search Algorithm

A sequential search on an ordered list usually requires you to search about half of the list. As the length of the list grows, the expected search time grows in direct proportion. For long, ordered lists, a *binary search* is much faster than a sequential search.

Binary search takes advantage of the fact that the list is ordered. First, the search item is compared with the middle element of the list. If the value of the middle element is equal to that of the search item, the search is complete. Otherwise, because the list is ordered, the algorithm repeats, searching either the first half or the last half of the list. This process is repeated using successively smaller parts of the list until either the search item is found or the part of the list being searched contains no more items.

Each time the search item is compared with a list element, the part of the list that remains to be searched is cut in half. The number of times that a list of n items can be cut in half is approximately equal to $\log_2 n$. Because every iteration of the binary search loop makes two item comparisons, the search will take at most $2 * \log_2 n + 2$ comparisons, total. That is, as the length of the list grows, the number of comparisons grows *logarithmically*. For example, the length of the list used in earlier exercises in this chapter is 20. 2^4 is 16, and 2^5 is 32; so, you can expect the binary search to make, at most, four or five iterations through its loop when searching for a value. By comparison, you could expect the sequential search to make about 20 / 2, or 10, iterations.

Objectives

In this lab, you use a binary search on an ordered list of a given size to find a particular value. Indicate whether the item is found. If it is, indicate the location where the item is found.

After completing this lab, you will be able to:

- Use a binary search on an ordered list of a given size for a particular value.

- Report if an item is found in the ordered list.

- If the item was found, report the location in the list where it was found.

Estimated completion time: **40–50 minutes**

Implementing the Binary Search Algorithm

In the following exercises, you revise the radio caller program you created in Lab 10.2 to use a binary search algorithm.

1. a. Continue working with the program that determines the winning caller to a radio show by revising the program you created in Lab 10.2 to determine which caller number wins the prize and the amount of the prize awarded. Use the binary search algorithm and the **prizeNos.srt** file you created in Lab 10.2.

   Make your search a "smart search" by first checking to see whether the value is less than the first element in the list or greater than the last element in the list. If the value falls within the range of the list, then the list should be searched. Include an output line that shows how many comparisons it takes to search for each guess.

   You should have the same screen results as those in Lab 10.1. An additional output message also appears, depending on the data entered. If the guess is less than the smallest number or greater than the largest number on the list, the following message should be displayed:

   ```
   It took 0 comparisons to check the list.
   ```

All other guesses will display one of the following messages:

`It took 4 comparisons to check the list.`

or

`It took 5 comparisons to check the list.`

Write your design in the following space. Your design should be a list of Java comments without any code.

1. b.   Implement the new design in Java. Save the program as **Prize3.java** to the device or location specified by your instructor. Compile, run, and test the program. After executing your program, select and copy everything that appears on your screen. Paste the copied text into a comment block at the end of your program.

Lab 10.4 Using the Class Vector

One of the limitations of arrays is that, when you create an array, its size remains fixed. Also, inserting or removing an element in the array at a specific position usually requires the program to shift the elements of the array that follow the insertion or deletion point.

In addition to arrays, Java provides the class `Vector` to implement a list. A `Vector` object can grow and shrink during program execution, as needed. Every element of a `Vector` object is a reference variable of the type `Object` that stores the address of any object, so you can store the reference of the object holding the data into a `Vector` element. Values of primitive data types cannot be directly assigned to a `Vector` element; you first must wrap the primitive data type element into an appropriate wrapper class.

The class `Vector` defines various methods for manipulation. The class `Vector` is contained in the package `java.util.Values`.

Objectives

In this lab, you become acquainted with the class `Vector` and various members of the class `Vector` to create a list in sorted order.

After completing this lab, you will be able to:

- Create objects of the `Vector` class.

- Use various members of the class `Vector`.

- Wrap a primitive data type element into an appropriate wrapper to be used as a `Vector` object.

Estimated completion time: **50–60 minutes**

Using the Class Vector

In the following exercises, you design and write a program using the class `Vector`.

1. a. *Critical Thinking Exercise*: Design a program to read values from a file into a `Vector` in sorted order. Create a file named **Numbers.txt** with the 20 unsorted values that you used in Lab 10.1. After all values have been entered and stored into the `Vector` object, display the contents of the vector to the screen.

   Following is a copy of the screen results that might appear after running your program, depending on the data entered. Your unsorted values:

   42
   468
   335
   1
   170
   225
   479
   359
   463
   465
   206
   146
   282
   329
   462
   492

496
443
328
437

Your sorted vector:

1
42
146
170
206
225
282
328
329
335
359
437
443
462
463
465
468

Write your design in the following space. Your design should be a list of Java comments without any code.

1. b. Save the program as **BuildList.java** to the device or location specified by your instructor. Compile, run, and test the program. After executing your program, select and copy everything that appears on your screen. Paste the copied text into a comment block at the end of your program.

LAB 10.5 USING String METHODS

Java provides various `String` methods to manipulate individual characters of a `String` object as well as substrings of the object. The class `String` is contained in the package `java.lang`.

Objectives

In this lab, you use `String` methods to search a string for the occurrence of a substring and replace it with another substring.

After completing this lab, you will be able to:

- Search a string for the occurrence of a substring.

- Replace a substring in a string with another substring.

- Change uppercase and lowercase characters to match the uppercase and lowercase use of the substring.

> Estimated completion time: **50–60 minutes**

Using String Methods

In the following exercises, you design and write programs that use `String` methods.

1. a. *Critical Thinking Exercise*: In this exercise, you design a search and replace program for a word processor. Ask the user to enter a string, a substring to search for within the string, and a substring to replace the search substring. Disregard the cases of the substrings. Use the case of the original string in the newly created string.

   Following is a copy of the screen results that might appear after running your program, depending on the data entered. The input entered by the user is shown in bold. Note that the program does not recognize that "instructer" actually should be "instructor".

   ```
   This program simulates the search and replace feature of a word
   processor. The user enters a sentence, a substring for which
   to search, and a substring to use for substitution.

   Please enter the string.
   Your teacher will assign a "Teach the Teacher" project for you to
   teach.

   Please enter the search string.
   teach

   Please enter the replacement string.
   instruct

   Your new sentence is:
   Your instructer will assign an "Instruct the Instructer" project for
   you to instruct.
   ```

Write your design in the following space. Your design should be a list of Java comments without any code.

1. b. Save the program as **Search.java** to the device or location specified by your instructor. Compile, run, and test the program. After executing your program, select and copy everything that appears on your screen. Paste the copied text into a comment block at the end of your program.

CHAPTER

11

INHERITANCE AND POLYMORPHISM

In this chapter, you will:

♦ Learn about inheritance
♦ Learn about subclasses and superclasses
♦ Explore how to override the methods of a superclass
♦ Examine how constructors of superclasses and subclasses work
♦ Learn about polymorphism
♦ Learn about composition

CHAPTER 11: ASSIGNMENT COVER SHEET

Name _____   Date _____

Section _____

Lab Assignments	Grade
Lab 11.1 Overriding Methods of the Superclass and Using Constructors of Subclasses and Superclasses	
Lab 11.2 Accessing Protected Members of the Superclass (Critical Thinking Exercises)	
Lab 11.3 Designing and Writing an Application Program Using Inheritance (Critical Thinking Exercises)	
Lab 11.4 Differentiating public, private, and protected Members of a Superclass	
Lab 11.5 Polymorphism (Critical Thinking Exercises)	
Total Grade	

See your instructor or the introduction to this book for instructions on submitting your assignments.

Lab 11.1 Overriding Methods of the Superclass and Using Constructors of Subclasses and Superclasses

You can create new classes from existing classes. You do not need to change the existing class directly; instead, you can inherit members of a class when designing another class. *Inheritance* is the characteristic that lets you create classes from existing classes. The new classes are called *subclasses*, and the existing classes are called *superclasses*.

Each subclass can be a superclass for a future subclass. In *single inheritance*, the subclass is derived from a single superclass; in *multiple inheritance*, the subclass is derived from more than one superclass. Java supports single inheritance, that is, a Java class can extend the definition of only one class. The general syntax of deriving a new class from an existing class follows:

```
modifier(s) class ClassName extends ExistingClassName modifiers(s)
{
memberList
}
```

The private members of the superclass are private members of the subclass, which means that the members of the subclass cannot directly access them. The subclass can *override*, or redefine, the public member methods of the superclass. The redefinition applies only to the objects of the subclass.

A subclass can have its own constructor. The constructors of the subclass can directly initialize only the instance variables of the subclass. When a subclass object is instantiated, the subclass object must also automatically execute one of the constructors of the superclass to initialize its (private) instance variables. A call to a constructor of the superclass is specified in the definition of a subclass constructor by using the reserved word `super`.

Objectives

In this lab, you define subclasses by extending superclasses.

After completing this lab exercise, you will be able to:

- Write a subclass by extending the superclass.

- Create instance variables of the subclass and the superclass.

- Recognize the difference between instance variables of the subclass and instance variables of the superclass.

- Use a constructor of a subclass to access the constructor of the superclass.

Estimated completion time: **120–150 minutes**

Overriding Methods of the Superclass and Using Constructors of Subclasses and Superclasses

In the following exercises, you examine a UML diagram, and then design and create a Java program based on this diagram.

1. a. Figure 11-1 shows a UML diagram for the class DateRec.

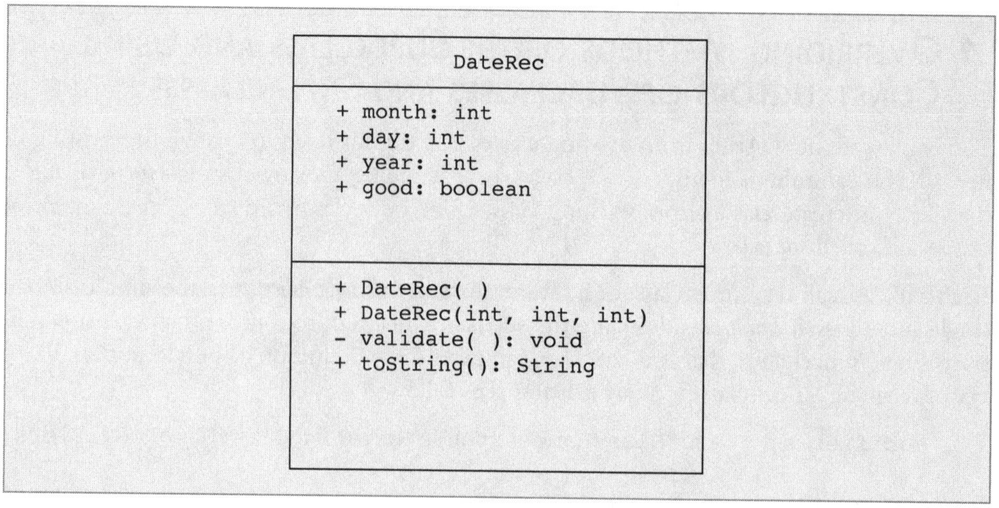

```
                        DateRec

            + month: int
            + day: int
            + year: int
            + good: boolean


            + DateRec( )
            + DateRec(int, int, int)
            - validate( ): void
            + toString(): String
```

Figure 11-1   UML diagram of the class DateRec

Create a DateRec class using the UML diagram shown in Figure 11-1 to write a Java class. The DateRec class should include the following elements:

- A default constructor that assigns the values 1, 1, and 2008 to the appropriate instance variables of the object, and assigns the value `true` to the instance variable `good`.

- A constructor that accepts values for `month`, `day`, and `year` through the parameter list, and assigns to the instance variable `good` the value returned from calling the method `validate()`.

- A method `validate()` that verifies whether the values of the instance variables `month`, `day`, and `year` are within proper ranges, and assigns `true` or `false` to the instance variable `good` depending on whether the other values are valid.

- A method `toString()` that formats as a `String` object the values for `month`, `day`, and `year`, and returns the `String`.

Write your class design in the following space. Your design should be a list of Java comments without any code.

1. b. Write your class and name it **DateRec.java**. Save the program to the device or location specified by your instructor.

Compile your class to be used later. (You cannot run your class code because you have not written a program to test the operations of the class DateRec.)

1. c. Design a program with a `main` method to test the DateRec class. The program should:

- Include comments for documentation and identification of the program in your design.

- Create a local variable named today, and assign to it a new object of the type DateRec created using the current date for month, day, and year.

- Create a local variable anyDay, and assign to it a new object of the type DateRec created with no arguments.

- Create a local variable noDay, and assign to it a new object of the type DateRec created with invalid date values.

- Call the `toString()` method for each DateRec object and display the values returned.

Following is a copy of the screen results that might appear after running your program, depending on the data entered.

```
You entered an invalid date: 02/29/1900

12/23/2004
01/01/2006
02/29/1900
```

Write your design in the following space. Your design should be a list of Java comments without any code.

1. d. Write a Java program based on the design that you created in Exercise 1c. For readability, insert blank lines to separate parts of the program. Include comments to explain the different sections of code.

Save the program as **DateTest.java** to the device or location specified by your instructor. Compile, execute, and test the program. Copy the output that is displayed, and paste it in a block comment at the end of your program. Then print your program to submit with your work.

2. a. Create a UML diagram for a class named Animal, described by the following:

- Include private integer values named `lifeExpectancy` and `weight`.

- Include a character value named `gender` and a string value called `name`.

- Allow for a public string value called `type`.

- Design an `Animal()` constructor with parameters to accept values for each data member.

- Design a public `void` method named `printValues()` with no parameters that displays all data members for the object of the Animal class.

Create your UML diagram in the following space.

2. b. Use the UML diagram for Animal that you created in Exercise 2a to design a Java class. Write your class design in the following space. Your design should be a list of Java comments without any code.

2. c. Enter your class and name it **Animal.java**. Save the program to the device or location specified by your instructor. Compile your class to be used later.

2. d. Design a program with a `main` method to test the Animal class. Your program should:

- Include comments for documentation and identification of the program in your design.

- Create a local variable named `elephant`, and initialize it with a new object of the type Animal. For the value of `gender`, use 'm' for male, 'f' for female, 'n' for a neutered male, or 's' for a spayed female. You can expect a male elephant to live 65 years and weigh around 7 tons (14,000 pounds).

- Call the `printValues()` method to display the instance variables of the object.

Following is a copy of the screen results that might appear after running your program, depending on the data entered.

```
A male elephant named Jumbo should live to be 65 and weigh 14000 pounds.
```

Write your design in the following space. Your design should be a list of Java comments without any code.

2. e. Write a Java program based on the design that you created in Exercise 2d. For readability, insert blank lines to separate parts of the program. Include comments to explain the different sections of code.

Save the program as **AnimalTest.java** to the device or location specified by your instructor. Compile, execute, and test the program. Copy the output that is displayed and paste it in a block comment at the end of your program. Then print your program to submit with your work.

3. a. Create a UML diagram for a subclass named Pet that extends the class Animal and includes the following elements:

- A string value named `home` and a Boolean value named `bites` as private instance variables

- A `Pet( )` constructor with parameters to initialize all data members of the class and to call the `Animal( )` constructor

- A `void` method named `printValues( )` with no parameters that displays all data members for the object of that class and then calls the `printValues( )` method of the Animal class to display the private data members of the superclass

Create your UML diagram in the following space

3. b. Use the UML diagram for Pet that you created in Exercise 3a to design a Java class. Write your class design in the following space. Your design should be a list of Java comments without any code.

3. c.   Enter your class and name it **Pet.java**. Save the program to the device or location specified by your instructor. Compile your class to be used later.

3. d.   Design a program with a `main` method to test the Pet class. Your program should:

- Include comments for documentation and identification of the program in your design.

- Create a local variable named dog, and initialize it with a new object of the type Pet. You can expect a spayed dog to live 11 years and weigh around 20 pounds. Your dog should live indoors and not bite.

- Call the method `printValues()` to display the data members of `dog`.

Following is a copy of the screen results that might appear after running your program, depending on the data entered.

```
A spayed dog named Fifi should live to be 11 and weigh 20 pounds.

Your dog lives indoors and does not bite.
```

Write your design in the following space. Your design should be a list of Java comments without any code.

3. e. Write a Java program based on the design that you created in Exercise 3d. For readability, insert blank lines to separate parts of the program. Include comments to explain the different sections of code.

Save the program as **PetTest.java** to the device or location specified by your instructor. Copy the output that is displayed, and paste it in a block comment at the end of your program. Then print your program to submit with your work.

Lab 11.2 Accessing Protected Members of the Superclass

Recall that there are four visibility categories for the members of a class: default (or package visibility), public, private, and protected. The private members of a class are directly accessible only by the methods of that class. The public methods are directly accessible by the methods of any class. Sometimes you want to provide direct access to the members of a superclass by the methods of that class and its subclasses, while preventing direct access by methods of other classes. To do this, you declare the superclass members using the modifier `protected`. In a UML class diagram, the pound symbol (#) is used to indicate that a member is protected.

Inheritance is one way to relate two classes, and *composition* is another way. Composition occurs when one or more members of a class are objects of another class type; that is, when an object of one class is *composed* of objects of another class.

Objectives

In this lab, you access protected members of the superclass from its subclass and write a subclass that uses composition.

After completing this lab, you will be able to:

■ Access protected members of the superclass from its subclass.

■ Use composition in a subclass.

> Estimated completion time: **60–90 minutes**

Accessing Protected Members of the Superclass

In the following exercises, you revise a UML diagram, class design, and related code to access protected members of a superclass.

1. Change your UML diagram, class design, and code for the Animal class to make the data member `name` public and the remaining data members protected instead of private. Also write a default Animal2 constructor containing no instructions. Save your changed class as **Animal2.java**, revise your code to reflect that change, and recompile your class. Change the class design and code for your **AnimalTest.java** program to test the Animal2 class. Save your changed program as **AnimalTest2.java**, and then recompile and run the program. Compare the results from **AnimalTest.java** and **AnimalTest2.java**. They should be the same.

2. a. *Critical Thinking Exercise*: Write a UML diagram for the subclass named VetPatient that extends the class Animal2. Include the following elements in the program:

   ■ The private instance variables `dateIn` and `dateOut` of the class type DateRec, `charges` of the data type `double`, and a `procedure` of the class type `String`

   ■ A constructor with parameters to initialize all data members of the class and to call the Animal2 constructor

   ■ A `void` method named `printValues()` with no parameters that displays all data members for the object of that class and then calls the `printValues()` method of the Animal2 class to display private data members of the superclass

   ■ Formats money amounts to show two decimal places

Create your UML diagram in the following space.

2. b. Use the UML diagram for VetPatient that you created in Exercise 2a to design a Java class. Write your class design in the following space. Your design should be a list of Java comments without any code.

2. c. Enter your class and name it **VetPatient.java**. Save the program to the device or location specified by your instructor. Compile your class to be used later.

2. d. Design a program with a `main` method to test the VetPatient class. Your program should:

- Include comments for documentation and identification of the program in your design.

- Create a local variable named `horse`, and initialize it with a new object of the type VetPatient. You can expect a spayed, female racehorse to live 25 years, weigh around 1,000 pounds, and have regular exams by a veterinarian.

- Call the method `printValues( )` to display the data members of `horse`.

Following is a copy of the screen results that might appear after running your program, depending on the data entered.

```
A spayed horse named Pretty Filly should live to be 25 and weigh
1000 pounds.

The horse checked in 8/30/2006 and checked out 8/31/2006.
The procedure performed was a check-up at a cost of $58.00.
```

Write your design in the following space. Your design should be a list of Java comments without any code.

2. e.   Write a Java program based on the design that you created in Exercise 2d. For readability, insert blank lines to separate parts of the program. Include comments to explain the different sections of code.

Save the program as **VetTest.java** to the device or location specified by your instructor. Copy the output that is displayed, and paste it in a block comment at the end of your program. Then print your program to submit with your work.

LAB 11.3 DESIGNING AND WRITING AN APPLICATION PROGRAM USING INHERITANCE

One advantage of using inheritance is the ability to reuse code that already has been tested for accuracy. This requires a program to test the class so that it can be reused. Test programs should access each data member and method of the class. After the class is tested, you can write a subclass that extends the superclass.

Objectives

In this lab, you design and write a subclass extending the Animal2 class and an application program that uses the subclass.

After completing this lab, you will be able to:

- Design a subclass extending a superclass to perform a particular purpose.

- Design and write an application program with a user-defined subclass.

Estimated completion time: **60–90 minutes**

Designing and Writing an Application Program Using Inheritance

In the following exercises, you create a UML diagram, and design and write a Java program that uses inheritance.

1. a. *Critical Thinking Exercise*: Create a UML diagram for the class named VetOffice that extends the superclass Animal2. The subclass VetOffice will be used by an application program you are to write for a veterinary practice.

   The class VetOffice should contain the following elements:

   - Public data members `double charges` and `int service`

   - Private data members `int days`, `String type`, and `char gender`

   - A `Boolean` method `initialize()` that has an `int` array parameter `costs`

   - A public `void` method `printValues()` that has parameters `today` of type DateRec and a `String` array `messages`

   The method `initialize()` performs the following tasks:

   - Continue to prompt the user for a service number until a valid service number is entered. (A valid service number is in the range of 0 through 15, inclusive.)

   - If the user enters a service number of 15 (other), prompt the user for the charge for the service.

   - If the user enters a service number of 4 (boarding), continue to prompt the user for the number of days boarding until a positive number of days is entered, and calculate the charge for boarding as 18 times the number of days.

   - If the user enters a service number other than 15 or 4, look up the charge in the table of costs.

   - Prompt the user for the name of the pet.

   - Continue to ask the user whether the pet is a dog or a cat until the user enters one of the two. If another pet type is entered, display a message stating that the practice is limited to dogs and cats.

   - Continue to prompt the user for the gender of the pet until a valid gender is entered.

The method `printValues()` is used to display a message showing the service performed; the gender, species, and name of the pet; the date of service; the service number; the service description; and the cost of service.

Create your UML diagram in the following space.

1. b.   Use the UML diagram for VetOffice to write a Java class. Write your design in the following space. Your design should be a list of Java comments without any code.

1. c. Enter your class and name it **VetOffice.java**. Save the program to the device or location specified by your instructor.

See the following Exercise 1d for the format and wording of messages to the user.

Compile your class to be used later.

1. d. Design an application program named VetBooks. Include comments for documentation and identification of the program in your design. Your program should:

- Prompt the user for today's date.

- Display the instructions to use the program and repeat instructions when requested.

- Create a daily output report file named **patients.txt** with the day's procedures. The daily output report includes a title with the clinic name, today's date, and column headings for patient, service, and fees.

- Calculate the total daily fees and output the total to the daily output report.

Following is a copy of the screen results that might appear after running your program, depending on the data entered. The user is first prompted for today's date.

```
Healthy Pet Clinic Daily Transactions
Please enter today's date separated by spaces (mm dd yyyy):
12 2 2005
```

The instructions should resemble the following:

```
The Healthy Pet Clinic offers services for your cats and dogs.

 1   Anesthesia                  $40
 2   Annual cat inoculations     $75
 3   Annual dog inoculations     $60
 4   Boarding per night          $18
 5   Check-ups                   $40
 6   Declawing                   $75
 7   Dog grooming                $75
 8   Nail or claw clipping        $8
 9   Neutering                   $50
10   Spaying                     $75
11   Worming                     $10
12   Surgery type 1             $100
13   Surgery type 2             $200
14   Surgery type 3             $300
15   Other
 0   Quit
```

The following prompts should appear until the user enters a 0 to end the program or until a valid procedure number has been entered.

```
Please enter the number of the service that you wish: 2
Please enter the name of your pet: Ferdinand
Please enter whether your pet is a cat or a dog: cat
Please enter the gender of your pet (m)ale, (f)emale, (s)payed,
(n)eutered: n
Would you like to see the instructions (y)es or (n)o: n
```

If an invalid service number is entered, the following message and prompt should be displayed until a valid procedure number is entered.

```
You entered an invalid procedure.
Please enter the number of the service that you wish: 2
```

If a 15 is entered as the procedure number, the following prompt should appear.

```
Please enter the cost of this procedure: 85
```

If an invalid pet type is entered, the following message and prompt should be displayed until a valid pet type is entered.

```
This practice is limited to dogs and cats.
Please enter whether your pet is a cat or a dog: cat
```

If an invalid gender type is entered, the following message and prompt should be displayed until a valid gender type is entered.

```
You did not enter a valid gender.
Please enter the gender of your pet (m)ale, (f)emale, (s)payed,
(n)eutered: n
```

If procedure 4 (boarding per night $18) is chosen, the following prompt should appear.

```
How many days do you wish to board? 1
```

If a positive number is not entered, the following message and prompt should be displayed until a positive number is entered.

```
You entered an invalid number of days.
```

For each patient that comes in, a message similar to the following one should appear, depending on the input data.

```
The following services were performed on your neutered cat Ferdinand:
12/02/2005      2  Annual cat inoculations      at a cost of $75.00.
```

The output file **patients.txt** should resemble the following report, depending on the data entered.

```
          The Healthy Pet Clinic Services for 12/02/2005

     Patient                    Service                    Fees
     --------------------       ---------------------------    -------
     Bowser               1  Anesthesia                  $40.00
     Ferdinand            2  Annual cat inoculations     $75.00
     Fifi                 3  Annual dog inoculations     $60.00
     Rover                4  Boarding per night          $54.00
     Harvard              5  Check-ups                   $40.00
     Sweetie              6  Declawing                   $75.00
     Isabel               7  Dog grooming                $75.00
     Tia                  8  Nail or claw clipping        $8.00
     Spot                 9  Neutering                   $50.00
     Fluffy              10  Spaying                     $75.00
     Gretchen            11  Worming                     $10.00
     Heinrich            12  Surgery type 1             $100.00
     Lucky               13  Surgery type 2             $200.00
     Zachery             14  Surgery type 3             $300.00
     Fido                15  Other                       $20.00

     Total                                            $1182.00
```

Write your design in the following space. Your design should be a list of comments without any Java code.

1. e.   Write a Java program based on the design that you created in Exercise 1d. For readability, insert blank lines to separate parts of the program. Include comments to explain the different sections of code. Save the program as **VetBooks.java** to the device or location specified by your instructor. Compile, run, and test the program with input that tests all cases. Copy the instructions, input, and output that are displayed (along with the contents of the file patients.txt), and paste them in a block comment at the end of your program.

LAB 11.4 DIFFERENTIATING public, private, AND protected MEMBERS OF A SUPERCLASS

A protected member of a superclass is public to the subclass, but private outside of the subclass and the superclass. By using the protected specifier, you can create a class member that can be inherited and accessed but remain private otherwise.

Objectives

In this lab, you become acquainted with the differences among public, private, and protected modifiers for accessing members of a superclass. You also learn about the inheritance of these specifiers.

After completing this lab, you will be able to:

- Differentiate public, private, and protected modifiers of members of a class.

Estimated completion time: **20–30 minutes**

Differentiating public, private, and protected Members of a Superclass

The following exercises are designed to demonstrate your understanding of the differences among public, private, and protected modifiers of members of a class so that you are better prepared to design and write programs that use protected members of a class in inheritance.

1. Show by example how a subclass inherits from a superclass.

2. What members of the superclass are included in the subclass?

3. Can a subclass inherit public members of the superclass as private members of the subclass?

4. If so, how are these members accessed in the subclass?

5. Can a subclass inherit private members of the superclass as public members of the subclass?

6. How are these members accessed in the subclass?

7. Can a subclass inherit protected members of the superclass as public members of the subclass?

8. How are these members accessed in the subclass?

9. Can a subclass inherit public members of the superclass as protected members of the subclass?

10. Can a subclass inherit protected members of the superclass as private members of the subclass?

LAB 11.5 POLYMORPHISM

Polymorphism literally means "multiple forms". In Java programming, polymorphism is based on the ability to associate an object of a subclass with a reference to its superclass. If the subclass redefines a method defined in the superclass, then calling the method using a superclass reference will invoke the method implementation of the object that actually is referenced.

A common application of polymorphism is to maintain an array of superclass references, each of which actually may refer to a superclass object or an object of any subclass object. Later, if the program needs to know the type of the object referenced by one of the array elements, the `instanceof` operator can be applied to it. The `instanceof` operator is a Boolean operator that reveals whether a reference actually refers to an object of a particular class.

When a superclass reference actually refers to a subclass object, a *downward cast* operation can be used to convert the superclass reference to a reference of the appropriate subclass.

Objectives

In this lab, you learn about polymorphism in Java.

After completing this lab, you will be able to:

- Assign subclass objects to a superclass reference variable.

- Use superclass reference variables properly, based on the type of the object referenced.

- Use the `instanceof` operator to determine the type of the object referenced by a reference variable.

Estimated completion time: **30–50 minutes**

Polymorphism

In the following exercises, you revise some earlier classes, write a program that demonstrates polymorphism, and then modify that program to use the `instanceof` operator.

1. a.   Modify the code for the Animal class so that it neither declares nor uses the weight and life expectancy data members. Save your changed class as **AnimalPoly.java** to the device or location specified by your instructor. Compile the class for later use.

1. b.   Modify the code of the Pet class so that it neither declares nor uses the home data member, and so that its superclass is AnimalPoly. Save your changed class as **PetPoly.java** to the device or location specified by your instructor. Compile the class for later use.

2. a.   *Critical Thinking Exercise*: Design a program that asks the user how many animals they have. For each animal, ask whether it is a pet or some other animal; based on the user's response, query the user for information needed to create the appropriate type of object to represent the animal. After data for all animals has been read, iterate through the array to print the animal objects.

If the user gives an invalid response when asked whether the animal is a pet or some other animal, inform the user and ask them to try again.

Design two methods in addition to `main`:

- `readAnimal` has one formal parameter, the Scanner object that represents the console. It asks the user to enter gender, name, and type values for the animal. The method then creates and returns an AnimalPoly object using the values entered.

- `readPet` has one formal parameter, the Scanner object that represents the console. It asks the user to enter gender, name, type, and bite values for the pet. The method then creates and returns a PetPoly object using the values entered.

Be sure to include comments and display the results to the user.

Following is a copy of the screen results that might appear after running your program, depending on the data entered. The input entered by the user is in bold.

```
How many animals do you have? 3

Enter 'p' for a pet, or 'o' for other: p
Gender (M, F, S, or N): M
Name: Comet
Type: dog
Bites (true or false)? true

Enter 'p' for a pet, or 'o' for other: x
Invalid response; please try again.
Enter 'p' for a pet, or 'o' for other: o
Gender (M, F, S, or N): F
Name: Liz
Type: lizard

Enter 'p' for a pet, or 'o' for other: p
Gender (M, F, S, or N): N
Name: Boxer
Type: cat
Bites (true or false)? False


Here is a summary:

A male dog named Comet
Your dog bites

A female lizard named Liz

A neutered cat named Boxer
Your cat does not bite
```

Write your design in the following space. Your design should be a list of Java comments without any code.

2. b. Write a Java program based on the design you created in Exercise 2a. Save the program as **AnimalList.java** to the device or location specified by your instructor. Compile, run, and test the program. Copy the instructions, input, and output that are displayed, and then paste them in a block comment at the end of your program.

3. a. Modify the code you created for PetPoly in Exercise 1b to include a new method:

   ■ getBites is an accessor method that returns the value of the bites data member.

   Save your changed class as **PetPoly2.java** to the device or location specified by your instructor. Compile the class for later use.

3. b. Modify the program you created in Exercise 2b to use class PetPoly2 rather than class PetPoly. Modify the print loop in the main method so that it calls the **getBites** accessor method only for the PetPoly objects in the array, accumulating a count of the number of pets that bite. After the loop is finished, print the count.

   Following is a copy of the screen results that might appear after running your program, depending on the data entered. The input entered by the user is in bold.

```
How many animals do you have? 3

Enter 'p' for a pet, or 'o' for other: p
Gender (M, F, S, or N): M
Name: Comet
Type: dog
Bites (true or false)? true

Enter 'p' for a pet, or 'o' for other: x
Invalid response; please try again.

Enter 'p' for a pet, or 'o' for other: o
Gender (M, F, S, or N): F
Name: Liz
Type: lizard

Enter 'p' for a pet, or 'o' for other: p
Gender (M, F, S, or N): N
Name: Boxer
Type: cat
Bites (true or false)? False


Here is a summary:

A male dog named Comet
Your dog bites

A female lizard named Liz

A neutered cat named Boxer
Your cat does not bite

1 of your pets bite.
```

   Save the program as **AnimalList2.java** to the device or location specified by your instructor. Compile, run, and test the program. Copy the instructions, input, and output that are displayed, and then paste them in a block comment at the end of your program.

HANDLING EXCEPTIONS AND EVENTS

In this chapter, you will:

- Learn what an exception is
- Learn how to use a `try/catch` block to handle exceptions
- Become acquainted with the hierarchy of exception classes
- Learn about checked and unchecked exceptions
- Learn how to handle exceptions within a program
- Discover how to throw and rethrow an exception
- Learn how to handle events in a program

CHAPTER 12: ASSIGNMENT COVER SHEET

Name _____ Date _____

Section _____

Lab Assignments	Grade
Lab 12.1 Catching Exceptions and Processing Exceptions During Program Execution Using try, catch, and catch Blocks (Critical Thinking Exercises)	
Lab 12.2 Combining catch Blocks Using the Operator instanceof	
Lab 12.3 Using Exception-Handling Techniques (Critical Thinking Exercises)	
Lab 12.4 Creating Your Own Exception Classes	
Lab 12.5 Using Event Handling (Critical Thinking Exercises)	
Total Grade	

See your instructor or the introduction to this book for instructions on submitting your assignments.

LAB 12.1 CATCHING EXCEPTIONS AND PROCESSING EXCEPTIONS DURING PROGRAM EXECUTION USING try, catch, AND catch BLOCKS

Until now, your programs have not included code to handle exceptions. If exceptions occurred during program execution, the program terminated with an appropriate error message. However, there are times that you don't want the program to simply ignore the exception and terminate.

One common way to provide exception-handling code is to add such code at the point where an error might occur. Java provides a number of exception classes. The class Throwable, which is derived from the class Object, is the superclass of the class Exception and contains various constructors and methods. Some methods, such as `getMessage`, `printStackTrace`, and `toString`, are public and so are inherited by the subclasses of the class Throwable.

Java's predefined exceptions are divided into two categories—*checked exceptions* and *unchecked exceptions*. Any exception that can be detected by the compiler is called a checked exception. For example, IOExceptions are checked exceptions. Enabling the compiler to check for these types of exceptions reduces the number of exceptions that are not handled properly by the program. The `throws` clause of a method header lists the types of exceptions that can be thrown by the method. The syntax of the `throws` clause is:

```
throws ExceptionType1, ExceptionType2, ...
```

where *ExceptionType1*, *ExceptionType2*, and so on are the names of the exception classes.

Those exceptions that the Java compiler might not be able to detect, such as *divide by zero* or *index out of bounds*, are called unchecked exceptions. These exceptions are descendant classes of the class RuntimeException.

Statements that might generate an exception can be placed in a `try` block. The `try` block also may contain statements that should not be executed if an exception occurs. The `try` block is followed by zero or more `catch` blocks. A `catch` block specifies the type of exception it can catch and contains an exception handler. The last `catch` block might or might not be followed by a `finally` block. Any code contained in a `finally` block always executes, regardless of whether an exception occurs. If a `try` block has no `catch` block, then it must have the `finally` block.

Objectives

In this lab, you catch exceptions that should be caught and process them during program execution.

After completing this lab exercise, you will be able to:

- Catch exceptions that should be caught.

- Process caught exceptions during program execution.

- Use multiple `catch` blocks for multiple exceptions of different types in the same program.

Estimated completion time: **90–120 minutes**

Catching Exceptions and Processing Exceptions During Program Execution Using try and catch Blocks

In the following exercises, you revise a program to catch and process exceptions.

1. a. *Critical Thinking Exercise*: In Chapter 11, you wrote a program called VetBooks that writes a daily report to a file. Redesign the VetBooks program to meet the following criteria:

   - If your output file is written to the hard disk, change the path to write your output file to removable media, such as a flash drive.

- Place `try` and `catch` blocks in a loop that continues until the user selects the option to quit.

- Implement a `catch` block for the FileNotFoundException exception that is thrown when the program cannot write to the specified output device (for example, when the removable media is not present). Allow the user to insert the removable media and continue program execution.

- Implement a `catch` block for the InputMismatchException exception that is thrown when the user enters nonintegral data for the service date. Allow the user to reenter the data in the proper format.

- Create Boolean values to keep track of whether the output file has been opened after an exception has been thrown and whether the date has been entered.

- Test to see if the date is valid. (Recall that the class DateRec has a public Boolean member **good** that indicates whether the date falls within a valid date range.) If the date is not valid, allow the user to reenter the date.

Following is a copy of the screen results that might appear while running your program when the removable media is not present.

```
Unable to open file; please connect media and press Enter to continue.
```

Following is a copy of the screen results that might appear if the date is entered with nonintegral data.

```
Your data was not in the correct format; please try again.
```

When your removable media is connected and the date is entered correctly, your output should match the same output as your VetBooks program, depending on the data entered.

Write your design in the following space. Your design should be a list of Java comments without any code.

1. b. Write a Java program based on the design you created in Exercise 1a. Save the program as **VetBooksEx.java** to the device or location specified by your instructor. Compile, execute, and test the program. Copy the instructions, input, and output that are displayed, and paste them in a block comment at the end of your program. Then print your program to submit with your work.

LAB 12.2 COMBINING catch BLOCKS USING THE OPERATOR instanceof

You can use the instanceof operator to determine if a reference variable points to an object of a particular class. You can combine multiple catch blocks into a single catch block and then use the instanceof operator to determine which exception was thrown.

Objectives

In this lab, you combine multiple catch blocks into one catch block and use the operator instanceof to determine which exception was thrown.

After completing this lab, you will be able to:

- Combine multiple catch blocks into one catch block.

- Use the operator instanceof to determine which exception was thrown.

Estimated completion time: **20–30 minutes**

Combining catch Blocks Using the Operator instanceof

In the following exercises, you design and write a program using the instanceof operator.

1. a. Change the class design for your **VetBooksEx** program to combine your multiple catch blocks in a single catch block. Use the instanceof operator to determine which exception was thrown. Your output should match the output of your **VetBooksEx** program, depending on the data entered.

    Write your design in the following space. Your design should be a list of Java comments without any code.

1. b. Write a Java program based on the design you created in Exercise 1a. Name your output file **patients2.txt**. Save the program as **VetBooks2.java** to the device or location specified by your instructor. Compile, execute, and test the program. Copy the instructions, input, and output that are displayed, and paste them in a block comment at the end of your program. Then print your program to submit with your work.

LAB 12.3 USING EXCEPTION-HANDLING TECHNIQUES

A catch block either handles an exception, or it partially processes the exception and then rethrows the same or another exception for the calling environment to handle.

You might have multiple try and catch (or finally) blocks in a program. Multiple methods could each have try and catch blocks. Java keeps track of the sequence of method calls. The public method printStackTrace can be used during program development to determine the order in which the methods were called and where an exception was handled.

When an exception occurs, the program can terminate, include code to recover from the exception, or log the error and continue.

Objectives

In this lab, you identify common exceptions NumberFormatException, IOException, and FileNotFoundException caused by user error and allow the user to continue.

After completing this lab, you will be able to:

- Write multiple try and catch blocks in multiple methods.

- Catch FileNotFoundException and allow the user to reenter the filename and continue.

- Catch NumberFormatException and allow the user to reenter the data and continue.

Estimated completion time: **120–150 minutes**

Using Exception-Handling Techniques

In the following exercises, you design and write a program that uses exception-handling techniques.

1. a. *Critical Thinking Exercise:* Two common errors users make when running a program are entering the incorrect type of data or forgetting to connect removable media for file output. Design a program that surveys a customer for their age, state, and zip code.

    Prompt the customer for their age. If they enter an age that is not an integral value, it means that they do not want to participate in the survey. Use a try block to detect this situation, and a catch block to display a message telling the customer that you understand they do not want to participate.

    If the customer enters their age, it means that they do want to participate in the survey. Prompt them for the name of a file that contains standardized, two-character abbreviations for each state, along with the names of the states. Use a try block to detect the situation in which the file cannot be opened, and a catch block to display a message telling the customer that the file cannot be opened. Read the contents of the file into a 50-row × 2-column array.

    Prompt them for the standardized, two-character abbreviation of their home state. Compare the value they enter against the contents of the state information array. Prompt the user for their five-digit zip code. Use a try block to detect the situation in which the zip code entered is not an integral value, and a catch block to display a message to the customer.

    Display the customer's age, state name, and zip code, and display a message telling the customer that their participation is valuable.

    Use a finally clause associated with the first try block to display a message that thanks the customer for participating in the survey.

Because you might be accessing some variables both within and outside specific `try` blocks, you must declare these variables before entering that `try` block. *Hint:* To declare the input file, use

```
Scanner inFile = null;
```

You will test your program several times with the keyboard input shown in the following list; your tests should produce the screen results shown, depending on the data entered:

- When the customer enters no value for age:

  ```
  Please enter your age or 'q' to quit:
  You've chosen not to participate. Thank you for your time.
  ```

- When the customer enters a character value for age:

  ```
  Please enter your age or 'q' to quit: q
  You've chosen not to participate. Thank you for your time.
  ```

- When the customer enters a valid value for age, an invalid filename, and "quit":

  ```
  Please enter your age or 'q' to quit: 20
  Please enter the name of your file or enter quit: nofile
  Unable to open file, please connect media, enter quit, or reenter
  the filename.

  Please enter the name of your file or enter quit: quit
  Your participation has been valuable. Thank you for your time.
  ```

- When the customer enters a valid value for age; a valid filename, **states.txt** (a file that can be found with your Chapter 12 student files); an invalid state two-character abbreviation, followed by a valid state two-character abbreviation; and an invalid zip code, followed by another invalid zip code, followed by a valid zip code:

  ```
  Please enter your age or 'q' to quit: 20
  Please enter the name of your file or enter quit: states.txt
  Please enter the 2 letter state abbreviation or quit: WS
  Your state abbreviation is not valid.
  Please enter the 2 letter state abbreviation or quit: TX
  Please enter your zip code: abc
  Invalid zip code; please reenter.
  Please enter your zip code: 123456
  Invalid zip code; please reenter.
  Please enter your zip code: 78734

  Your age: 20
  Your state and zip: Texas 78734
  Your participation has been valuable. Thank you for your time.
  ```

Write your design in the following space. Your design should be a list of Java comments without any code.

1. b.   Write a Java program based on the design you created in Exercise 1a. For readability, insert blank lines to separate parts of the program. Include comments to explain the different sections of code. Save the program as **Address.java** to the device or location specified by your instructor. Compile, run, and test the program with input that tests all cases. Copy the instructions, input, and output that are displayed, and paste them in a block comment at the end of your program.

LAB 12.4 CREATING YOUR OWN EXCEPTION CLASSES

Java provides a substantial number of exception classes, but does not provide all the exception classes that you will ever need. Java's mechanism to process the exceptions you define is the same as that for built-in exceptions. However, you must throw your own exceptions using the `throw` statement.

The exception class that you define must extend either the class Exception or one of its subclasses. If you have created an exception class, you can define still other exception classes extending the definition of the exception class you created.

Objectives

In this lab, you create your own exception class, import the class into your program, and throw and catch the exception.

After completing this lab, you will be able to:

- Create your own exception class extending the class Exception.

- Throw an exception of the type you create.

Estimated completion time: **60–90 minutes**

Creating Your Own Exception Classes

In the following exercises, you revise a program that includes exception classes that you create.

1. a. In Chapter 9, you wrote a program called Trucks that compares a truck's weight to an established maximum weight limit and displays a message to tell the user whether the truck is within weight limits. Redesign the Trucks program to throw a checked exception when a truck's weight exceeds the limit. To accomplish this, write your own exception class; the constructor of your exception class should call the constructor of its superclass (Exception), passing it as an argument the message shown in Figure 12-2, below. Write a `try` block in which you throw an object of your exception class when the weight limit of a truck is exceeded. Write a `catch` block that catches the thrown object and displays its message in a dialog box. Add a second `catch` block to catch NumberFormatException exceptions when invalid numeric data is entered. Incorporate a loop into your program so that your program can continue after exceptions are caught.

    Depending on the data entered, your screen results should be identical to the screen results for your Trucks program in Chapter 9, except for the additional message for invalid data. Figure 12-1 shows the screen result that should appear when no data or nonnumeric data is entered. Figure 12-2 shows the screen result that should appear when the weight limit is exceeded.

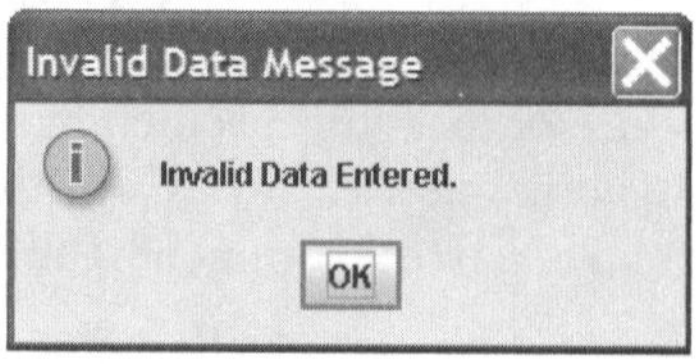

Figure 12-1   Invalid Data Message

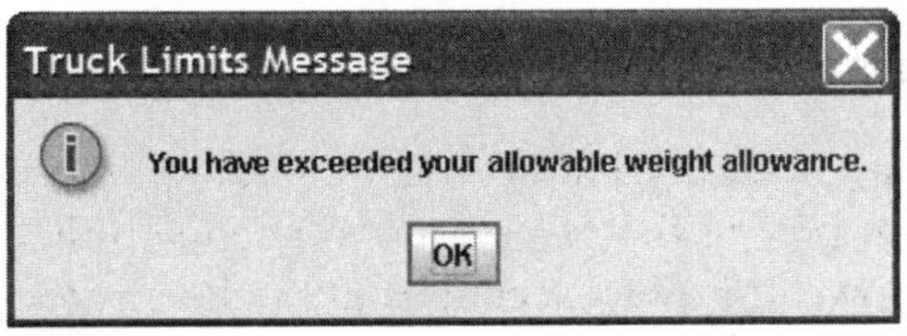

Figure 12-2   Weight exceeded message

Write your design in the following space. Your design should be a list of Java comments without any code.

1. b.   Write a Java program based on the design you created in Exercise 1a. Save the exception class as **WeightLimitException.java** and the program as **Trucks2.java** to the device or location specified by your instructor. Compile, execute, and test the program. Either copy the dialog boxes that appear and paste them into a document or print the screens of the dialog boxes. Then print your program to submit with your work.

LAB 12.5 USING EVENT HANDLING

An event is a specific action that triggers predefined code. Java provides various interfaces to handle different events. For example, when an action event occurs, the method `actionPerformed` of the interface ActionListener is executed. To create an object to handle an event, first you create a class that implements an appropriate interface.

One way to handle events in a program is to use *anonymous classes*. To register an action listener object to a GUI component, you use the method `addActionListener`. To register a window listener object to a GUI component, you use the method `addWindowListener`. The WindowListener object being registered is passed as a parameter to the method `addWindowListener`.

The following example creates an object of an anonymous class, which extends the class Window-Adapter and overrides the method `windowClosing`. The object created is passed as an argument to the method `addWindowListener`. The method `addWindowListener` is invoked by explicitly using the reference `this`.

```
this.addWindowListener(new WindowAdapter()
        {
            public void windowClosing(WindowEvent e)
            {
             System.exit(0);
            }
        }
    );
```

Objectives

In this lab, you use buttons to generate an action event and implement the interface ActionListener.

After completing this lab, you will be able to:

- Organize a GUI application using the methods `setSize` and `setLocation`.

- Use buttons to generate an action event.

- Implement the interface ActionListener.

Estimated completion time: **60–90 minutes**

Using Event Handling

In the following exercises, you design and write a program that uses event handling.

1. a. *Critical Thinking Exercise*: Design a program to calculate a monthly loan payment and the total amount to be paid over the life of a loan. Ask the user for the amount of the loan, the interest rate, and the number of months of the loan. The user should click a button to perform the calculations and another button to reset the input and output fields. Format your GUI with labels identifying each field and buttons for calculations and to reset the fields. The actual layout is up to you to design.

The formula for calculating a loan payment is:

```
payment amount = (principle*rate/12*Math.pow(rate/12+1, time)) /
                 (Math.pow(rate/12+1, time)-1);
```

Figure 12-3 shows the Loan Payment dialog box at the start of the program and immediately after the Reset button is clicked:

Figure 12-3   Loan Payment dialog box at the beginning of the program

Figure 12-4 shows the Loan Payment dialog box after the user has entered valid amount, interest, and month information:

Figure 12-4   Loan Payment dialog box after user enters correct data and clicks Calculate

Figure 12-5 shows the Loan Payment dialog box after the user has entered an incorrect amount, interest, or months:

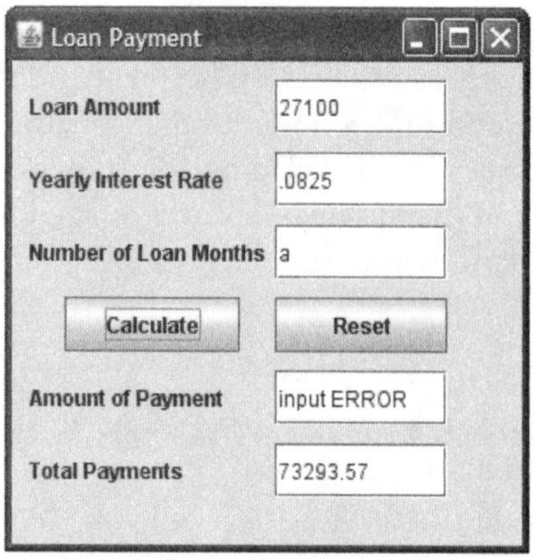

Figure 12-5   Loan Payment dialog box after user enters incorrect data and clicks Calculate

Write your design in the following space. Your design should be a list of Java comments without any code.

1. b.   Write a Java program based on the design you created in Exercise 1a. Save the program as **LoanPay.java** to the device or location specified by your instructor. Compile, execute, and test the program. Either copy the dialog boxes that appear and paste them into a document or print the screens of the dialog boxes. Then print your program to submit with your work.

ADVANCED GUIs AND GRAPHICS

In this chapter, you will:

♦ Learn about applets

♦ Explore the class `Graphics`

♦ Learn about the class `Font`

♦ Explore the class `Color`

♦ Learn to use the additional layout managers

♦ Become familiar with more GUI components

♦ Learn how to create menu-based programs

♦ Explore how to handle key and mouse events

Chapter 13: Assignment Cover Sheet

Name _____   Date _____

Section _____

Lab Assignments	Grade
Lab 13.1 Creating a Java Applet Containing Formatted Strings	
Lab 13.2 Creating a Java Applet Containing Shapes (Critical Thinking Exercises)	
Lab 13.3 Converting an Application Program to an Applet	
Lab 13.4 Using Additional GUI Components (Critical Thinking Exercises)	
Lab 13.5 Using Lists in Various Layouts and Using Menus	
Lab 13.6 Reviewing Key Events and Using Mouse Events	
Total Grade	

See your instructor or the introduction to this book for instructions on submitting your assignments.

LAB 13.1 CREATING A JAVA APPLET CONTAINING FORMATTED STRINGS

In Java, an *applet* is a Java program that is embedded in a Web page and executed by a Web browser. The class is declared public and is created by extending the class JApplet, which is contained in the package javax.swing.

A Java applet is referenced by an HTML page, which includes tags that tell a browser how to interpret the HTML code. The code to be formatted is written between opening and closing tags that are not case sensitive, though it is recommended that you use uppercase letters. An opening tag is written between left and right angle brackets, as in `<TITLE>`. A closing tag is written with a left-angle bracket, a slash, the command, and a right-angle bracket, as in `</TITLE>`. Not all code requires closing tags; in fact, the browser ignores nonessential closing tags. Incorrectly written tags also are ignored.

An HTML comment begins with a left angle bracket and an exclamation mark, and ends with a dash and a right angle bracket, as in `<!--Java applet code starts here.-->`.

Use the following tags to create HTML pages for testing your Java applets:

```
<HTML>
<HEAD>
<TITLE>
            Your page name to be displayed in the title bar
</TITLE>
</HEAD>

<BODY>
            <!--Include your instruction to include your applet code.-->

<APPLET code = "NameOfApplet.class" width = "numberOfPixels"
height = "numberOfPixels">
</BODY>
</HTML>
```

Unlike Java application programs, Java applets do not have the method `main`. However, you compile applets the same way that you compile any other Java program. When a browser runs an applet, the methods `init`, `start`, `paint`, `stop`, and `destroy` are guaranteed to be invoked in sequence. To use the various methods of the class `Graphics`, you need to import the java.awt package.

You use the `init` method to perform the following tasks:

■ Initialize variables.

■ Get data from the user.

■ Place various GUI components.

The `paint` method has one argument, which is a Graphics object, and is used to perform output. The `init` and `paint` methods need to share common data items, so these common data items are the data members of the applet class. The method `drawString` displays the `String` value specified by its first argument at the horizontal position *x* pixels away from the upper-left corner of the applet, and the vertical position *y* pixels away from the upper-left corner of the applet, as specified by the second and third arguments, respectively.

To show text in different fonts, you use an object of the class `Font`, contained in the package java.awt. You specify the font face name, style, and size expressed in points, where 72 points equal one inch. For example, the following code creates a 12-point italic font named Serif:

```
new Font("Serif", Font.ITALIC, 12)
```

The following code creates a 36-point italic and bold font named Dialog:

```
new Font("Dialog", Font.ITALIC + Font.BOLD, 36)
```

Java provides the class `Color` in the package java.awt to change the color of text or the background of a component. The color scheme—known as *RGB* (Red/Green/Blue)—is used to mix the amounts of red, green, and blue hues to represent any color. These hue values are represented by integers in the range of 0 through 255, inclusive. The value 0 means no amount of the color indicated will be used. For example, the value for white is 255, 255, 255 and the value for black is 0, 0, 0. The gray color 100,100,100 is darker than the gray color 200, 200, 200.

Objectives

In this lab, you create a Java applet and the HTML page to contain the applet.

After completing this lab exercise, you will be able to:

- Create an HTML page that calls an applet.

- Create a Java applet that displays formatted strings.

- Format strings for font face, style, size, and color.

- Use a Java applet to create a cover sheet for your programs.

Estimated completion time: **50–60 minutes**

Creating a Java Applet Containing Formatted Strings

In the following exercises, you design and write a Java applet that contains formatted text.

1. a. Design a Java applet that creates a cover sheet you can use to submit your programs to your instructor. Use the following `Font` face names, styles, sizes, and colors to identify your chapter title, name, class section, and assignment date (or any other information required by your instructor):

- Font names: Times New Roman, Courier, Arial, and Dialog

- Font styles: bold, plain, italic, and bold italic

- Font sizes: 42, 30, 24, and 18 points

- Font colors: red, blue, green, and orange

Following is an example of one screen result that appears after running appletviewer with your HTML page depending on the font face, style, and size chosen.

Figure 13-1   Cover applet

Write your design in the following space. Your design should be a list of Java comments without any code.

1. b. Write a Java class based on the design you created in Exercise 1a, and name it **Cover.java**. Save the program to the device or location specified by your instructor.

   Compile your class to be used later. (You cannot run your class code because you have not created an HTML page to activate your applet.)

1. c. Create an HTML page that invokes the applet Cover.class. Save your page as **Cover.htm** to the device or location specified by your instructor. Run the appletviewer with your Cover.htm page or open your page in a browser. Either copy the Applet Viewer dialog box that appears and paste it into a document, or print the screen that displays the HTML page.

LAB 13.2 CREATING A JAVA APPLET CONTAINING SHAPES

The class `Graphics` also provides methods for drawing items such as lines, ovals, rectangles, and polygons on the screen. For example, you use the method `drawLine` to designate the location of a line by specifying the *x*- and *y*-coordinates of the beginning point to the *x*- and *y*-coordinates of the ending point. You use the method `drawRect` to draw a rectangle by specifying the *x*- and *y*-coordinates of the upper-left corner, the width *w*, and the height *h* of the rectangle.

Objectives

In this lab, you design rectangles and an oval to create flags, and fill the shapes with the colors of a flag. You determine which flag is displayed by randomly generating a number in the range of 0 to 3 to display one of four different flags. Your completed flags should be three units wide by two units high.

After completing this lab, you will be able to:

- Create a Java applet that displays filled rectangles and ovals.

Estimated completion time: **50–60 minutes**

Creating a Java Applet Containing Shapes

In the following exercises, you design and write a Java program that draws shapes.

1. a. *Critical Thinking Exercise*: Create a Java applet that fills rectangles and an oval to represent flags. Use a pseudorandom number generator to determine which flag is presented. Use the following values:

   - 0 to present the French flag using three horizontal rectangles of the same size with the colors blue, white, and red (left-to-right).

   - 1 to present the Austrian flag using three vertical rectangles of the same size with the colors red, white, and red.

   - 2 to present the Spanish flag with three horizontal rectangles, in which the top and bottom rectangles are red and each fill 25 percent of the total rectangle. The center rectangle is yellow and fills 50 percent of the rectangle.

   - 3 to present the Bangladeshi flag, which is green with a red circle left of center.

   Figures 13-2 to 13-5 show examples of each flag in dialog boxes that appear after running appletviewer with your HTML page.

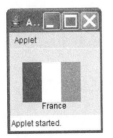

Figure 13-2   French flag

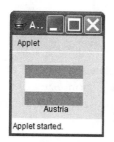

Figure 13-3   Austrian flag

Figure 13-4   Spanish flag

Figure 13-5   Bangladeshi flag

Write your design in the following space. Your design should be a list of Java comments without any code.

1. b. Write a Java class based on the design you created in Exercise 1a, and name it **Flags.java**. Save the program to the device or location specified by your instructor.

Compile your class to be used later. (You cannot run your class code because you have not created an HTML page to activate your applet.)

1. c. Create an HTML page that invokes the applet Flags.class. Save your page as **Flags.htm** to the device or location specified by your instructor. Run the appletviewer with your Flags.htm page several times or open your page in a browser until all options have executed. Either copy the AppletViewer dialog boxes that appear and paste them into a document, or print the screens that display the HTML pages.

LAB 13.3 CONVERTING AN APPLICATION PROGRAM TO AN APPLET

To convert a GUI application to an applet, you must do the following:

- Extend the definition of the class JApplet by changing JFrame to JApplet.
- Change the constructor to the method `init`.
- Remove method calls such as `setVisible`, `setTitle`, and `setSize`.
- Remove the method `main`.
- Remove the *Exit* button and all code associated with it, such as the action listener, and so on.

Objectives

In this lab, you convert a GUI application to an applet.

After completing this lab, you will be able to:

- Convert a GUI application to an applet.

Estimated completion time: **20–30 minutes**

Converting an Application Program to an Applet

In the following exercises, you revise Java programs you've already written so that they become graphical applets.

1. a.   Copy the **LoanPay** program from your Chap12 folder to the device or location specified by your instructor. Save the program as **LoanPay2.java**. Make the changes required to convert a GUI application to an applet.

Following is an example of one screen result that appears after running appletviewer with your HTML page depending on the data entered.

Figure 13-6 shows the dialog box displayed at the start of the program and after the Reset button is clicked.

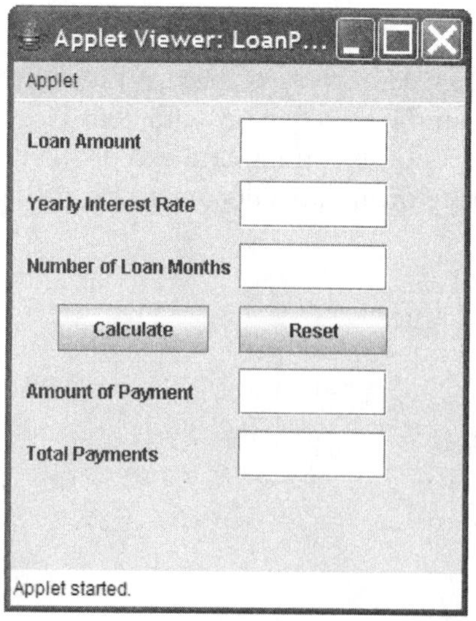

Figure 13-6   Loan payment GUI at start or reset

Figure 13-7 shows the dialog box displayed after the user has entered the amount, interest, and months.

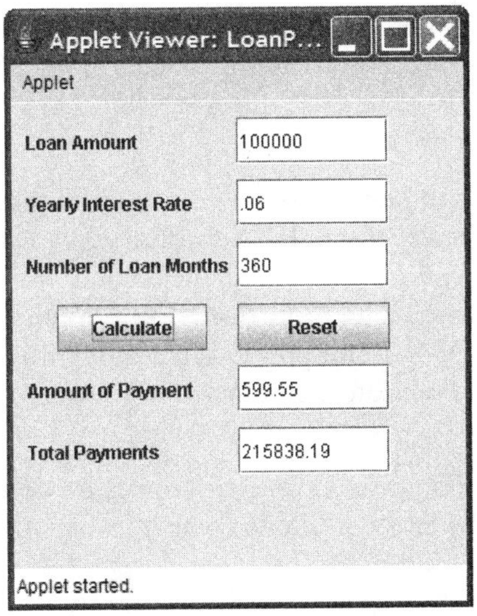

Figure 13-7   Loan payment GUI after calculation

Figure 13-8 shows the dialog box displayed after the user has entered an incorrect amount, interest, or months.

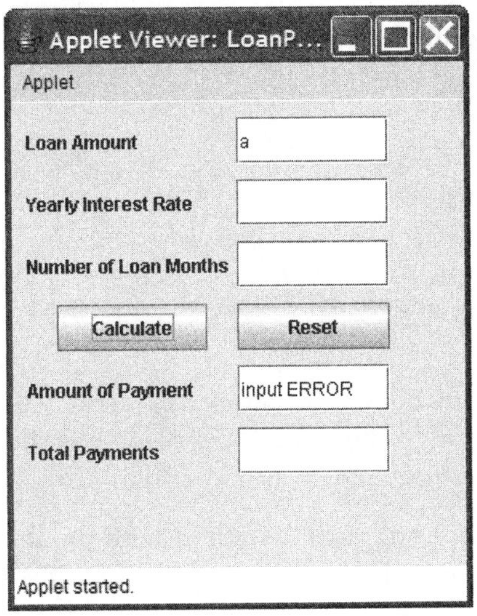

Figure 13-8   Loan payment GUI after input error

1. b.   Compile your class to be used later. (You cannot run your class code because you have not created an HTML page to activate your applet.)

1. c.   Create an HTML page that invokes the applet LoanPay2.class. Save your page as **LoanPay2.htm** to the device or location specified by your instructor. Run the appletviewer with your LoanPay2.htm page or open your page in a browser. Either copy the AppletViewer dialog boxes that appear and paste them into a document, or print the screen that displays the HTML page.

LAB 13.4 USING ADDITIONAL GUI COMPONENTS

Java provides additional GUI components to display and input data. The class JTextArea allows multiple lines for input and output. Other methods used with the class JTextArea include `setColumns()`, `setRows()`, `append()`, `setLineWrap()`, `setWrapStyleWord()`, and `setTabSize()`. Inherited methods include `setText()`, `getText()`, and `setEditable()`.

The JCheckBox and JRadioButton classes allow a user to select a value from a set of given values. Both of these classes are subclasses of the abstract class ToggleButton. To select or deselect a check box, you click the check box. When you click a JCheckBox, it generates an item event. Item events are handled by the interface ItemListener that contains the abstract method `itemStateChanged`. You can select multiple check boxes; however, you can select only one radio button in a group. To make sure that the user can select only one radio button at a time, you create a button group and group the radio buttons.

You use a *combo box*, commonly known as a *drop-down list*, to select an item from a list of options. A JComboBox generates an ItemEvent that is monitored by an ItemListener, which invokes the method `itemStateChanged` exactly as in JCheckBox or JRadioButton.

Objectives

In this lab, you become acquainted with the GUI components JTextArea, JCheckBox, JRadioButton, and JComboBox.

After completing this lab, you will be able to:

- Use a JTextArea, JCheckBox, JRadioButton, and JComboBox in an applet.

Estimated completion time: **180–210 minutes**

Using Additional GUI Components

In the following exercises, you work with different GUI components. Due to the time it takes to create the GUI layout, you are not required to test the data for validity.

1. a. *Critical Thinking Exercise*: Design a Java applet that provides a form to survey computer usage. After completing the form, the user should click the Submit button. A dialog box should show the user what was input. Create a Reset button so that the user can clear the form.

   Hint: To reset the JComboBox, use the `setSelectedItem()` method with the first element of the list. You can choose any layout you want. The form should include the following elements:

   - Text fields for first name, last name, street address, city, state, zip, e-mail, and computer store name

   - A combo box with a list of computer stores and a choice of "other"

   - Check boxes to select the type of computer

   - Radio buttons to select what is important in a computer purchase

   - A text area for comments

   Figures 13-9 to 13-11 show examples of the screen results that appear after running the appletviewer with your HTML page.

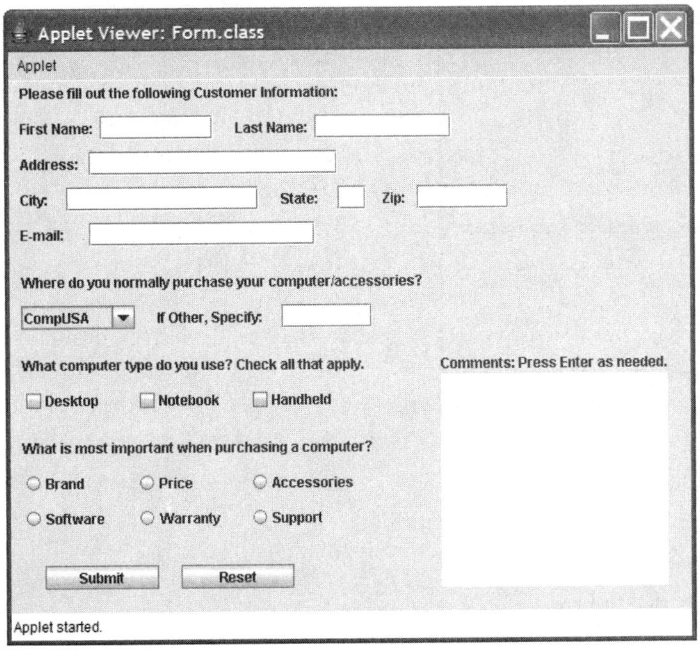

Figure 13-9   Computer survey form at start or at reset

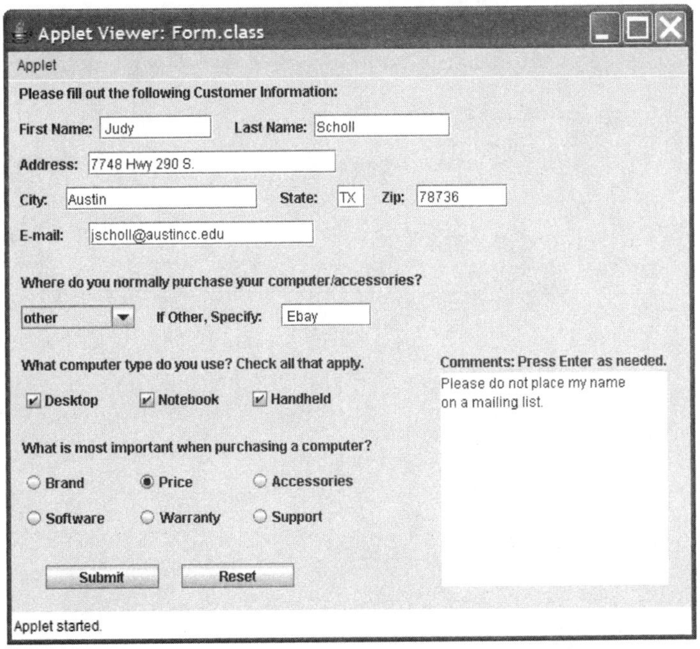

Figure 13-10   Completed computer survey form

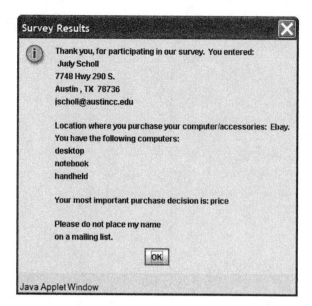

Figure 13-11 Survey Results dialog box

Write your design in the following space. Your design should be a list of Java comments without any code.

1. b.   Write a Java class based on the design you created in Exercise 1a, and name it **Form.java**. Save the program to the device or location specified by your instructor.

Compile your class to be used later. (You cannot run your class code because you have not created an HTML page to activate your applet.)

1. c.   Create an HTML page that invokes the applet Form.class. Save your page as **Form.htm** to the device or location specified by your instructor. Run the appletviewer with your Form.htm page or open your page in a browser. Either copy the Applet Viewer dialog boxes that appear and paste them into a document, or print the screens that display the HTML page.

LAB 13.5 USING LISTS IN VARIOUS LAYOUTS AND USING MENUS

A *list* displays a number of items from which the user can select one or more. Creating a JList is similar to creating a JComboBox. Like JComboBox, you can also designate the number of rows shown in a list and restrict the list to single selection.

You can select an item on a list and display an image corresponding to the item selected. To process a ListSelectionEvent, you use the interface ListSelectionListener. The interface has the method **valueChanged**. You can determine the index of the selected item by using the method **getSelectedIndex**. You use this index to select the corresponding image from the pictures array and the name of the image from the pictureNames array. Then you use the method repaint to repaint the pane.

Java provides many layout managers. You have already used GridLayout and **null**. Another layout is the default layout manager called FlowLayout. In GridLayout, all rows have the same number of components and all components have the same size. In FlowLayout, you can align each line either left, center, or right using a statement such as the following:

```
flowLayoutMgr.setAlignment(FlowLayout.RIGHT);
```

The default alignment is left.

The BorderLayout manager allows you to place items in specific regions. This manager divides the container into five regions: NORTH, SOUTH, EAST, WEST, and CENTER. NORTH and SOUTH span horizontally from one edge of the container to the other. EAST and WEST components extend vertically between the components in the NORTH and SOUTH regions. The component placed at the CENTER expands to occupy any unused regions. See Figure 13-12.

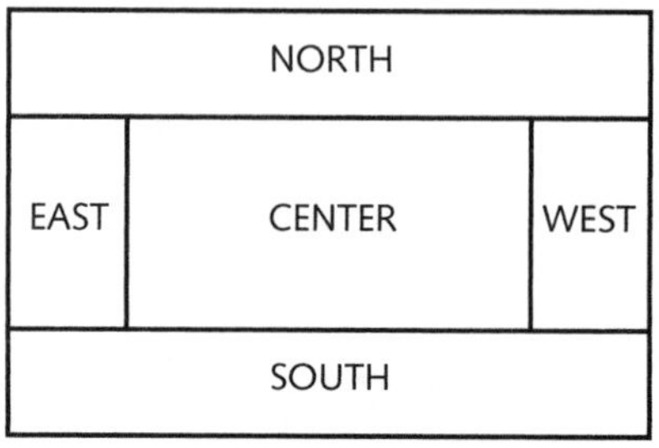

Figure 13-12   Five regions in the BorderLayout manager

Menus allow you to provide various options to the user without cluttering the GUI with too many components. The classes JFrame and JApplet both have a method setJMenuBar that allows you to set a menu bar. The order in which you add menus to the menu bar determines the order in which they appear.

Objectives

In this lab, you become acquainted with using lists in various layouts and with using a menu bar instead of a list.

After completing this lab, you will be able to:

- Write a program with a list using the **null** layout.

- Rewrite a program with a list using FlowLayout.

- Rewrite a program with a list using BorderLayout.

- Rewrite a program using a menu bar.

Estimated completion time: **120–150 minutes**

Using Lists in Various Layouts and Using Menus

In the following exercises, you work with different layouts.

1. a. Design a Java program that uses a list with the names of four different flags. Display the flag that corresponds with each list item when the item is clicked. Use the `null` layout and the four flag GIF files stored in the Chap13 folder of your student files; the GIF files are named **Italy.gif**, **Japan.gif**, **JollyRoger.gif**, and **US.gif**.

Figures 13-13 to 13-16 show the screen results that might appear after running your program depending on the sizes and locations that you choose.

Figure 13-13   Flag Viewer showing the U.S. flag

Figure 13-14   Flag Viewer showing the Italian flag

Figure 13-15   Flag Viewer showing the Jolly Roger flag

Figure 13-16   Flag Viewer showing the Japanese flag

Write your design in the following space. Your design should be a list of Java comments without any code.

1. b. Write a Java program based on the design you created in Exercise 1a. Save the program as **Flags2.java** to the device or location specified by your instructor. Compile, execute, and test the program by clicking each item in the list. Either copy the windows that appear and paste them into a document, or print the screens of the windows. Then print your program to submit with your work.

2. Rewrite the program you created in Exercise 1 to use FlowLayout. Save the program as **Flags3.java** to the device or location specified by your instructor. Compile, execute, and test the program by clicking each item in the list. Either copy the windows that appear and paste them into a document, or print the screens of the windows. Then print your program to submit with your work.

Figure 13-17 shows an example of one screen result that might appear after running your program.

Figure 13-17   Flag Viewer using FlowLayout

3. Rewrite the program you created in Exercise 1 to use BorderLayout. Save the program as **Flags4.java** to the device or location specified by your instructor. Compile, execute, and test the program by clicking each item in the list. Either copy the windows that appear and paste them into a document, or print the screens of the windows. Then print your program to submit with your work.

Figure 13-18 shows an example of one screen result that might appear after running your program.

Figure 13-18 Flag Viewer using BorderLayout

4. Rewrite the program you created in Exercise 1 to use a menu. Save the program as **Flags5.java** to the device or location specified by your instructor. Compile, execute, and test the program by clicking each item in the list. Either copy the windows that appear and paste them into a document, or print the screens of the windows. Then print your program to submit with your work.

Figure 13-19 shows an example of one screen result that might appear after running your program.

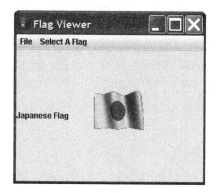

Figure 13-19 Flag Viewer using a menu

LAB 13.6 REVIEWING KEY EVENTS AND USING MOUSE EVENTS

In Chapter 12, you learned that when you press a key while the cursor is in a text field, an action event is generated. When you press a mouse button to click a button on a form, in addition to generating an action event, a mouse event is generated. Likewise, when you press the *Enter* key in a text field, in addition to the action event, a key event is generated. Therefore, a GUI program can simultaneously generate more than one event.

There are three types of key events. The interface KeyListener contains the methods `keyPressed`, `keyReleased`, and `keyTyped` that correspond to these events. When you press a *meta key* (such as *Control*, *Shift*, or *Alt*), the method `keyPressed` is executed; when you type a regular alphanumeric key, the method `keyTyped` is executed. When you release any key, the method `keyReleased` is executed.

A mouse can generate seven different types of events. The events `mouseClicked`, `mouseEntered`, `mouseExited`, `mousePressed`, and `mouseReleased` are handled by MouseListener. The events `mouseDragged` and `mouseMoved` are handled by the interface MouseMotionListener.

Objectives

In this lab, you become acquainted with using mouse events.

After completing this lab, you will be able to:

■ Display an image when the `mouseEntered` event occurs.

■ Display text when the `mouseExited` event occurs.

Estimated completion time: **50–60 minutes**

Reviewing Key Events and Using Mouse Events

In the following exercises, you design and write a program that displays an image in response to a mouse event.

1. a. Design a program that displays a label "Fat Cat." When a `mouseEntered` event occurs on the label, show only the image **fatcat1.gif**, which is stored in the Chap13 folder of your student files. When the `mouseExited` event occurs, show only the text "Fat Cat."

Figures 13-20 and 13-21 show examples of screen results that appear after running your program depending on the layout that you choose. (Fat Cat image is courtesy of Don Gosselin.)

Figure 13-20   Fat Cat text

Figure 13-21 Fat Cat image

Write your design in the following space. Your design should be a list of Java comments without any code.

1. b. Write a Java class based on the design you created in Exercise 1a, and name it **CatPic.java**. Save the file to the device or location specified by your instructor. Compile, execute, and test the program by moving the mouse cursor over the window and then moving the mouse cursor away from the window. Either copy the windows that appear and paste them into a document, or print the screens of the windows. Then print your program to submit with your work.

RECURSION

In this chapter, you will:

♦ Learn about recursive definitions

♦ Explore the base case and the general case of a recursive definition

♦ Learn about recursive algorithms

♦ Learn about recursive methods

♦ Learn how to use recursive methods to implement recursive algorithms

CHAPTER 14: ASSIGNMENT COVER SHEET

Name _____   Date _____

Section _____

Lab Assignments	Grade
Lab 14.1 Designing and Implementing a void Recursive Method	
Lab 14.2 Designing and Implementing a Value-Returning Recursive Algorithm (Critical Thinking Exercises)	
Lab 14.3 Using Recursive Methods Instead of Looping	
Lab 14.4 Using a Recursive Method as Part of an Expression (Critical Thinking Exercises)	
Total Grade	

See your instructor or the introduction to this book for instructions on submitting your assignments.

LAB 14.1 DESIGNING AND IMPLEMENTING A void RECURSIVE METHOD

One way to repeat code is through looping (or iterative) structures. Another method is called recursion. A *recursive method* is one that calls itself. A *recursive definition* is one in which something is defined as a smaller version of itself. Recursion, like a loop, stops when a certain condition is met. The condition that causes the recursive method to stop is called the *base case* of the recursive method.

In recursion, a set of statements is repeated by having the method call itself. Moreover, a selection control structure is used to control the repeated calls in recursion.

- Every recursive definition must have one or more base cases.

- The general case must eventually be reduced to a base case.

- The base case stops the recursion.

A recursive method in which the last statement executed is the recursive call is called a *tail recursive method*.

Objectives

In this lab, you design and implement a Java program that calls a void recursive method to reverse the elements of a string.

After completing this lab, you will be able to:

- Design and implement an algorithm to use a void recursive method.

- Use a recursive method for String processing.

Estimated completion time: **50–60 minutes**

Designing and Implementing a void Recursive Method

Suppose you want to reverse a String value. For instance, a String with a value of "Hello" would be displayed as "olleH". To help design the algorithm, first answer a few questions. Because all program designs need to consider input, processing, and output, start by determining how you want to accomplish these tasks.

1. How will the declaration of your reference variable look?

2. How will the value of the reference variable be input—as an assigned value or entered by the user?

3. Do you need to know the exact length or only the maximum length of the value of the reference variable?

4. What information (arguments) should the driver program pass to the recursive method?

5. How do you know when the recursive method has reached the base case?

6. Will you display the reversed reference variable element by element or as another reference variable?

7. If you send the reference variable and the length of the String to the recursive method, you always know the last element of the reference variable. What would you do to process a different last character of the reference variable each time?

8. a. Design a program that calls a recursive method to display a string in reverse order. Write your program design in the space provided. Your design should be a list of Java comments without any code.

Following is a copy of the screen results that might appear after running your program, depending on the data entered. The user's input appears in bold.

```
This program asks a user to enter a message.
The message is then displayed in reverse order.

Please enter a message: Hello

Your message in reverse is: olleH
```

8. b.   Write a Java program based on the design you created in Exercise 8a. Save the program as **Reverse.java** to the device or location specified by your instructor. Compile, execute, and test the program. Copy the instructions, input, and output that are displayed, and paste them in a block comment at the end of your program. Then print your program to submit with your work.

LAB 14.2 DESIGNING AND IMPLEMENTING A VALUE-RETURNING RECURSIVE ALGORITHM

If every recursive call results in another recursive call, the recursive method (algorithm) is said to have *infinite recursion*. Every call to a recursive method requires the system to allocate memory for the local variables, formal parameters, and information that allows control to be transferred back to the calling method. Infinite recursion will cause the system to run out of memory and abnormally terminate. Design your algorithms to meet the following criteria:

- Understand the problem requirements.

- Determine the limiting conditions.

- Identify the base cases and provide a direct solution to each base case.

- Identify the general case and provide a solution to each general case in terms of a smaller version of itself.

Objectives

In this lab, you design and write a Java program that uses a value-returning recursive method call instead of a looping structure.

After completing this lab, you will be able to:

- Design and implement an algorithm that uses a recursive call as part of a value-returning expression.

Estimated completion time: **50–60 minutes**

Designing and Implementing a Value-Returning Recursive Algorithm

Critical Thinking Exercise: Design a recursive algorithm to find the value of n raised to the power of x (or n^x). Design a program that calls a recursive method based on your algorithm. Your method should have arguments for the base, exponent, and answer, and should return the integer value answer. The base and exponent values must be integral values greater than or equal to zero. To help design the algorithm, first answer the questions in the following exercises.

Use a `try` block to parse the integer input. Use a `catch` block to end the recursion using the `InputMismatchException` exception, and use a `finally` block to return the answer from the recursive method.

Because all program designs need to consider input, processing, and output, answer the following questions to determine how you want to accomplish these tasks.

1. How will the values for your base and exponent be input—by assignment or by interactive input?

2. The driver program might restrict input to valid, numeric values. However, your method should accommodate all integer values. How will you accommodate negative exponents?

3. How will you accommodate zero exponents?

4. How will you accumulate the values returned from the recursive method?

5. How will you display the result from the method calls?

6. a. Design a program from the problem description. Write your design in the space provided. Your design should be a list of Java comments without any code.

   Following is a copy of the screen results that might appear after running your program, depending on the data entered. The user's input appears in bold.

```
This program asks a user to enter a base number and an exponent.
The answer is calculated and displayed.

Please enter your base number and your exponent (q to quit): 0 0
The number 0 raised to the power of 0 is 1.

Please enter your base number and your exponent (q to quit): 0 4
The number 0 raised to the power of 4 is 0.

Please enter your base number and your exponent (q to quit): 4 4
The number 4 raised to the power of 4 is 256.

Please enter your base number and your exponent (q to quit): 4 2
The number 4 raised to the power of 2 is 16.

Please enter your base number and your exponent (q to quit): q
Thank you for using the Power program.
```

6. b. Write a Java program based on the design you created in Exercise 6a. Save the program as **Power.java** to the device or location specified by your instructor. After executing your program, select and copy everything that appears on your screen. Paste the copied text into a comment block at the end of your program. Then, print your program to submit with your work.

LAB 14.3 USING RECURSIVE METHODS INSTEAD OF LOOPING

When designing a recursive method, consider that a recursive method executes more slowly than its iterative counterpart. On slower computers, especially those with limited memory space, the slow execution of a recursive method would be visible. On newer computers with a large amount of memory space, the execution of a recursive method usually is not noticeable.

A program design for a recursive method is very similar to a program design for a loop.

Objectives

In this lab, you redesign and implement a Java program that you previously wrote using loops.

After completing this lab, you will be able to:

- Design programs using recursive methods instead of loops.

Estimated completion time: **50–60 minutes**

Using Recursive Methods Instead of Looping

In the following exercises, you redesign and revise a program to use recursive methods instead of looping.

1. a.   In Lab 5.1, Exercise 3, you designed a repetition program named **Find1.java** to search an input file for a particular item. Refer to that design and redesign it to use a recursive method. Write your design in the space provided. Your design should be a list of Java comments without any code.

1. b. Copy the file **invoice1.dat** from your Chap05 folder into your Chap14 folder. Write a Java program based on the design you created in Exercise 1a. Save the program as **FindRecursive.java** to the device or location specified by your instructor. Compile, run, and test the program. Either copy the dialog boxes that appear and paste them into a document, or print screens of the dialog boxes. Depending on the data entered, your output should be identical to the output of your **Find1.java** program in Chapter 5.

   Test your program with the file **invoice1.dat** and with the following input:

   ```
   shovel
   ```

   Print your input file and program and attach them to your printed output screens to submit with your work.

LAB 14.4 USING A RECURSIVE METHOD AS PART OF AN EXPRESSION

When a statement calls a recursive method as part of an expression, it is a recursive call. The process of returning values back through the layers of recursive calls is known as *unwinding the recursion*.

Objectives

In this lab, you design and implement a Java program that uses a recursive call as part of an expression.

After completing this lab, you will be able to:

- Use Java to implement the design of an algorithm that uses a recursive call as part of an expression.

- Use the returned value from a recursive call to add to a value that is an accumulator.

> Estimated completion time: **50–60 minutes**

Using a Recursive Method as Part of an Expression

In the following exercises, you design and write a program that uses a recursive method to reverse the order of integers.

1. a. *Critical Thinking Exercise*: Design a program that uses a recursive method to reverse the order of integers. For example, if you have an integer with a value of 5982, the displayed integer should be 2895. Do not convert the integer to a `String` value to accomplish the task. You must calculate it as an integer. Display the starting number and the ending number.

   Following is a copy of the screen results that might appear after running your program, depending on the data entered. The user's input appears in bold.

   ```
   This program asks a user to enter a number.
   The number is then displayed in reverse order.

   Please enter a positive number (q to quit): 123456
   Your number 123456 written in reverse is 654321.

   Please enter a positive number (q to quit): 456543
   Your number 456543 written in reverse is 345654.

   Please enter a positive number (q to quit): 9807
   Your number 9807 written in reverse is 7089.

   Please enter a positive number (q to quit): 1
   Your number 1 written in reverse is 1.

   Please enter a positive number (q to quit): q
   Thank you for using the reverse number program.
   ```

   Write your design in the following space. Your design should be a list of Java comments without any code.

1. b. Write a Java program based on the design you created in Exercise 1a. Save the program as **IntReverse.java** to the device or location specified by your instructor. Compile, run, and test the program with the input shown in Exercise 1a. Copy the instructions, input, and output that are displayed, and then paste them in a block comment at the end of your program. Then, print your program to submit with your work.

Index

Special Characters

?: (conditional operator), 78-79
* (asterisk), 21, 35
&& (double ampersand), 65
== (double equal sign), 65
|| (double pipe), 65
++ (double plus sign), 25
> (greater than operator), 65
>= (greater than or equal to operator), 65
< (less than operator), 65
<= (less than or equal to operator), 65
! (logical not), 65
!= (not equal to operator), 65
% (percent sign), 21
+ (plus sign), 21, 28
# (pound symbol), 246
"" (quotation marks), 23
/ (forward slash), 21
- (minus sign), 21
// (double forward slash), 35
- - (double minus sign), 25

A

abstract data types (ADTs), 186–190
accessor methods, 186
action events, 130
action listener(s), 130
ActionListener interface, 275–278
`ActionPerformed` method, 130–131
activating methods, 43
`addActionListener()` method, 128
addition operator (+), 21
addresses, 4
  base, of array, 201
`addWindowListener` method, 275
ADTs (abstract data types), 186–190
algorithms. *See* method(s); *specific algorithms*
allocating memory, 24
ALU (arithmetic logic unit) , 4
American Standard Code for Information Interchange (ASCII), 7, 19
ampersand, double (&&), logical AND, 65

anonymous classes, 275
applets, 8, 9, 17
  converting application programs to, 288–289
  formatted strings, 281–284
  shapes, 285–287
application programs, 5, 8, 9, 17
  converting to applets, 288–289
  designing and writing using inheritance, 250–255
arithmetic logic unit (ALU), 4
arithmetic operators, 21–22
arrays, 191–213
  accessing individual elements, 193–195
  base address, 201
  binary search algorithm, 226–228
  declaring, 193–195
  dynamic, 193
  indexes. *See* index(es), arrays
  initializing, 196–200
  instantiating, 193–195
  multidimensional, 210–213
  of objects, 204–209
  parallel, 204–209
  passing as parameters to methods, 201–203
  processing, 193–195
  sequential search algorithm, 217–220
  sorting using selection sort, 221–225
  `String` methods, 232–234
  two–dimensional, 210–213
  `Vector` class, 229–231
ASCII (American Standard Code for Information Interchange), 7, 19
assembly language, 7
assignment, 24
assignment statements, 25, 36
asterisk (*)
  comments, 35
  import statements, 35
  multiplication operator, 21
attributes of windows, 125
Augusta, Ada, 3
auto–unboxing wrapper objects, 136
autoboxing primitive values, 136